THE WA

ABOUT THE AUTHOR

The 58 year-old co-author of *The Way It Was*, Nina Naudé, is the life partner of the golf pro Bobby Verwey, whose biography this is. They both retired to Ramsgate, Kwa-Zulu Natal, about three years ago, where they are enjoying a sea view, wonderful climate and trips to the many game reserves.

Having listened to all his stories over a period of time, Nina decided that it will give closure to so many things that have happened in his life; partly about the complicated relationship he had with Gary Player, his brother-in-law, but also all the humorous, sad and unheard of stories about golfers and what happened over a forty-year period.

With the help of freelance editor Lea Jacobs, who wrote South African soccer star Gary Bailey's biography, the book became a reality.

Nina Naudé has travelled extensively and her love for books and the written word has given life to this book and helped to put Bobby's memories on paper. She has written a few short stories in the past, but not much else. She also had her own gardening column in a Cape Town newspaper a few years ago.

She is in the process of opening her own photographic studio where she will express her love for people and children in another form.

Apart from her two children, it will be one of her biggest achievements to see a book she has spent so many hours on, on the shelves. In the process it will also give Bobby Verwey true recognition for what he has done in the golfing world.

BOBBY VERWEY Snr

The Way It Was

Revelations of a Golf Pro

by NINA NAUDÉ

AUSTIN MACAULEY
PUBLISHERS LTD.

A CIP catalogue record for this title is available from the
British Library.

ISBN: 978-1-78629-121-9 (paperback)
ISBN: 978-1-78629-122-6 (eBook)

www.austinmacauley.com

First Published (2016)

Austin Macauley Publishers Ltd.
25 Canada Square
Canary Wharf
London
E14 5LQ

ACKNOWLEDGEMENTS

Bob Crouch: Indianapolis, Indiana. When I first started playing in the States in 1960, he and his wife took me in like a long-lost son. They became my American parents. Gerty died more than a year ago, at the age of 96 and visiting Mr Crouch last year, I cannot believe how well he still is at the age of 96. Hopefully I will get to see him again before the year is out. I am eternally grateful for having had them in my life.

Gary Westwater and Joe Stravino: Two of the very best friends I ever had, who have always been there for me. Through good and bad times, I have always been able to count on them. Thank you, guys, for being there for me. Joe, you always find time to talk to me in your busy day. I really appreciate it more than you will ever know.

Mavis Hookum: I cannot say enough about her. She was my mother's best friend. Back in the early 'fifties she would pick me up at school, when we would play nine holes of golf. She became like a second mother to me. She passed away two or three years ago: may she rest in peace.

Jack Nicklaus and his wife, Barbara: They must be the most amazing people I have ever met. Always very nice towards me and my family; considering that he most probably is the greatest golfer ever, his humility is admirable. Some top golfers could take a leaf out of his book.

Herman Brown: Herman got me involved in horse racing and taught me all of what I know today. Through my friendship with him, I became associated with the great racehorse, 'Gate Crasher' – arguably the best racehorse South Africa has ever seen next to 'Horse Chestnut'. I taught his son, Herman Brown Junior, to play golf at the age of fourteen and a twenty-two handicapper. Five years later he became a plus two handicapper.

Jon Bredenkamp: My very best friend from school days. It bugs me to this day that I regrettably never invited you to my first wedding. Jon, old buddy, I forgot, it is that plain and simple, but I will always be your friend.

Tony Rivilland: Tony became my fourth son. Having been involved in racing for 57 years, I know that he is the best horse trainer in the country. Over the years he would tell me a horse could win and 48 times out of 50 the horse would win. I'm happy, to still have him in my life and that he still has time to answer my phone calls and incessant questions.

Brenda and Mike Osborne: Brenda and Mike, who lived in Kent, UK, were unbelievably good to me when I played in Britain. I will never forget their generosity when I was there, whether with a car, accommodation or just companionship.

Gordon Millar: I have to thank Gordon for always being there for me. He worked for me at the driving range for twenty years and assisted me whenever I needed it. I could not have done it without him. Gordy, you are a good man and I am very lucky to still call you my friend.

Andy Stubbs: He definitely warrants a mention. Head of the European Senior Tour, he has always been very pleasant to me and is still doing a great job on the tour.

Neville Sundleson: He was a great golfer and also won the World Amateur at one time, making me his daughter's godfather and for helping me whenever I needed him. Although we have lost contact along the way, I still count him as one of my best friends.

To my three sons, Bobby Junior, Bradley and Darren: You have always been a phone call away, and whether we have a discussion about horse racing, rugby, cricket or golf, it warms my heart that you still keep in touch with your old Dad. I love you all to the moon and back.

CONTENTS

FOREWORDS

F OR MANY years Bobby Verwey's main claim to fame was that he was Gary Player's brother-in-law. His sister, Vivienne, had married Player when they were both very young but after an almost meteoric rise to fame Player was a huge figure in the world of golf.

Bobby was talented, never the most powerful player, but blessed with a beautiful short game and a lively personality. In the early days he gloried in his position of being close to such an iconic figure as Player. He made the very most of his talents, won many tournaments and always looked very dapper.

Like a lot of families, over the years there has been discord as this book reports, but it's the tale of a traveller. Someone who got behind the scenes, where perhaps greater players never tread, listening to the gossip, the chat, the envies, the jealousies; his story is at times riveting. It certainly brings a different slant into the world of professional golf.

PETER ALLISS, Professional golfer and BBC Television presenter and commentator, author and golf course designer. Inducted to the World Golf Hall of Fame in May 2012.

WHEN ASKED to write a short paragraph for my father's book, it got me thinking. Should I talk about his prowess as an international golf pro, winning tournaments on three continents or should I mention the fact that I never saw him hurt a living soul? I could write a long story about that. No, I think, the real story about my Dad is one of what can happen when the principle of faith is applied.

When he found out he was exempt in the British Senior Open, he came to us and stated that he was going to win. Having not picked up a golf club in five years it was a laughable statement. To confess, we did laugh.

His steadfast belief, unwavering faith brought him victory. After that, the message was always: 'You've got to believe.' Faith, the evidence of things unseen. Always reminding me that there is a greater force at work. And if you just 'believe', Anything is possible…

FRANK ROBERT VERWEY JUNIOR (BOBBY)

AS A teenager, in the '70s, I only saw my dad play when he was on the Sunshine Tour in South Africa. In the '90s, when he was in the USA, I seldom saw him play. It was something my dad did that took him away from home for long periods of time. I did not really give it much thought as I was growing up.

It was only when he asked me to caddy for him in America that I really began noticing what a popular and well known guy he was. In 1994, I walked into the Clubhouse at Desert Mountain, Arizona and stood admiring the photos of some of their star players on the wall. Gary Player, Arnold Palmer, Jack Nicklaus, Lee Trevino and… Bobby Verwey… What!!? He was amongst all those greats that I have watched play for so long. It never, ever crossed my mind that he could be one of them. I was so proud to be on that golf course with him, watching how people loved his game, shouting his name. Then of course there were groupies following us around, checking him out, checking me out. At 25 years of age, I was definitely enjoying the attention of the fairer sex and there were some hotties around.

I remember one time, coming back to the hotel from an all nighter, where booze flowed like water. I was rudely awoken, after what felt like five minutes of sleep, at six o'clock in the morning by my dad. I was to caddy for him that day and he was not giving me any excuses for the hangover I had. Dragging the golf bag around, with a searing headache and legs that felt like lead. He did not allow me to take a golf cart to ease my suffering, but had me walk with him all the way. Only at the last hole was I allowed to get the clubs and my sorry ass on that cart and follow him around.

He was a hard taskmaster and I admire him for that. First one on the practice tee and the last one to leave at night. Being with him on tour made me realise how hard and how competitive it was. He was always friendly and talkative on the golf course, throwing a ball to a fan or signing a cap. His fans loved his easygoing manner, chatting to them with that baritone voice of his, never forgetting to acknowledge them. It was an awesome life, and I would not change it for anything.

I love you for that, Dad.

BRADLEY JAY VERWEY

WHEN I was asked to write a few words about my Dad, the first thing that came to mind was the times I went to America and Europe to caddy for him. I never for one minute thought how much hard work it was going to be. Playing every day and practising like he had something to prove to the world. To me he was already a champion in more ways than one.

After travelling for hours we would get to the course where he was going to play that week. No rest for the weary, but straight to the putting green or to the practice tee to try and find a few extra yards. His work ethic on the Senior tour was second to none. Not even my uncle, Gary Player, who my brother Bobby was caddying for at the time, could match that. When the pressure was on, he played to the best of his ability.

My dad always made sure we had the best of everything, especially golf equipment. Even when he realised that I was not going to follow in his footsteps. I never felt pressured to fill those amazing shoes. He has always supported me in any of my business ventures or personal decisions that I have made in my life.

Every morning starts with a telephone call and some discussion with my dad. Whether it is about horse racing, rugby, cricket or golf. I value his opinion so much and I thank him for always being there for me.

DARREN KEL VERWEY

INTRODUCTION

A LL MY life as a professional golfer, on and off the golf course, I was known as Bobby Verwey, Gary Player's brother-in-law. I would like to tell you a very important fact... He married *my* sister and therefore became without a doubt, *my* brother-in-law.

Although I had my own success and racked up forty-two top ten finishes in the USA, nobody really knew of these accomplishments back in South Africa, because of the lack of TV coverage in those days.

I also have to give credit to my father, Jock Verwey, three times South African PGA Tour champion, who I believe was never really acknowledged in a lot of golfers' success. He was a strong character and the foundation of my beliefs, my private life and my professional career. I know that he was extremely proud of my achievements.

This is the controversial, exciting, sad, most of all funny, but also true set of stories which transpired in the past sixty years, as I travelled the globe. I am a non-confrontational and gullible man, observing and unfortunately sometimes trusting the wrong people.

Folks who have met me and seen me play, or heard my booming voice across the golf course, will know me as a good and friendly guy, but sadly sometimes a little too opinionated. Therefore sometimes getting the short end of the stick, as you will see.

Crying in my scotch at the ripe old age of 74 is definitely not in my character. I want to relate mainly the humorous side of this special game called golf, more so than blowing my own trumpet.

This is also about all the amazing people I have met as well as a few well-known unsavoury characters and down right cheats in the golfing circles. Whether they like it or not, I am sure they will recognise themselves or see their name in my book. Some stories you may remember and some you most probably may never have heard of, but some you will most definitely not forget. Lessons learned… for sure, lessons taught… absolutely.

My family and friends are worried that relating some stories would be too controversial, stepping on hallowed ground… Even going as far as calling me a bitter old man. But as my brother-in-law once told me, it makes for good reading.

I hope you enjoy my book, I have been silent for far too long and now it is my turn to tell it… the way it was…

'The secret to life is attitude… ' Bobby Verwey

Chapter One

THE EARLY YEARS

I PUTTED the ball and before it even went in, I realised that I'd achieved my lifelong ambition – I'd won the Senior British Open Championship. It was 1991, I was 50 years old and had endured a number of setbacks in my career, but none of that mattered anymore: I had beaten some of the top players in the world – players I had known and played with for most of my life, players who had garnered my respect over the years and many of whom had supported me through the good times and when things got seriously tough.

Playing professional golf in the '60s was, if you'll pardon the pun, a completely different ball game when you compare it to how the players operate today. We were a close-knit bunch – and when I say close, I mean really close. We competed against one another and although the competition may have been as fierce as is it today, this didn't mean that we couldn't be friends off the course. There was the odd exception, but generally, we played together, stayed in the same hotels with our wives and families when we were on the circuit, and we had a bond, in my opinion, that was stronger than in any other sport at the time. The actual game of golf may not have changed over the hundreds of years it has been played, but the way professional players approach their game certainly has. Looking back, most of the players of that era relied on their natural talent. They may well have had coaches, but that didn't mean that they adopted the almost scientific approach that is so often seen in the sport today. The paparazzi, if it even existed at the time, didn't follow our every move on and off the course; in fact, the only people who really took an interest in the game were either die-hard golf supporters or those who caught the occasional game on television. I'm not suggesting that there wasn't a keen interest in the sport – there was, but there certainly wasn't the frenzied levels of attentiveness that the sport garners today, which, given some of our antics on and off the golf course, wasn't necessarily a bad thing.

I suppose, given my family's links to the game, that I was always destined to be a professional golfer.

My late father, Jock Verwey, who went on to win the South African PGA Championship three times, was the son of a farmer who worked in the North West Province of South Africa. One of eleven children, he grew up in an Afrikaans-speaking home and was forced like many other children of that time to attend an English-speaking boarding school when the family relocated to the Johannesburg area in what is now Gauteng. Unhappy and unable to speak in his mother tongue, he consistently ran away from school until he realised that he had to stay put until he was old enough to leave and get a job, which turned out to be in the Post Office.

While he may not have been that keen to study, he was mad about sport from an early age and went on to play rugby for the Wanderer's Rugby Club. He was also an avid long-distance runner – the love of which was undoubtedly based on his consistent efforts to run away from school.

He was first introduced to golf by his older brother, Pat, who asked him if he wanted to earn some pocket money by carrying a golf bag around the Parkview Golf Club. He leapt at the chance and was soon caddying 36 holes on a Saturday and 36 holes on a Sunday for the grand sum of two tickeys (less than a bit) per day.

Forced to wait for their money until the players had finished drinking after the game, my father and the other caddies would use the time to hunt for lost golf balls, which they would sell for extra cash. However, in order to keep the balls, the boys would go to a putting green on the 14th, which was illuminated by a street light, and have a sort of play off in order to see who would take the balls home. Unfortunately for my dad, he was a lousy putter and although he would religiously hunt for and find balls he would invariably lose them all to the other, more experienced caddies. Never a good loser, he decided to up the ante and when he was given a putter by a club member he focused all his attention on getting the ball into the hole. He practised for hours and it wasn't long before he was winning between 60 to 70 golf balls a time and selling them for around 4 Rand (approximately 33 US cents in today's money) on a weekly basis. He would hand the money over to my grandmother and although she gratefully accepted the extra cash, would swear that he was going to go to hell for doing such a wicked thing. For some reason she regarded the way in which my father earned the money as morally reproachable. Fortunately, my father didn't share her religious fervour and continued to contribute to the family's somewhat desperate financial circumstances for a number of years, using these so called ill-gotten gains.

It wasn't only the caddies who were drawn to the antics that took place on the 14th green. The action invariably drew a small crowd of interested spectators, including the woman who would go on to become his wife and my mother.

The determination to win those balls soon started to pay off and it wasn't long before my dad became an excellent golfer and a phenomenal putter. His abilities on the golf course did not go unnoticed and as such he was invited to play in the Transvaal Amateur Championship. He made it into the final and was pitted against a man by the name of Armour Mathews who came from a well-to-do family. As they walked onto the first tee, Mathews unwrapped a whole packet of new golf balls. My father, who at the time was still handing over most of his salary and any extra money that he earned to my grandmother, didn't have the cash to invest in new balls. However, he was determined to look the part and ceremoniously unwrapped the older balls that he had cleaned and wrapped in paper before taking his first shot. Unfortunately, he lost to Mathews on the last hole.

My father was the sort of person that aced anything he turned his hand to, although he sometimes made a decision that would land him in serious trouble. He was found in possession of unwrought gold when he worked on the mines. He was found guilty and sentenced to three years, but only spent fifteen months in the Pretoria Central Prison. He was a very likeable guy and they thought he had learned his lesson.

It's quite an amazing story that, forty years later, he bumped into a guy on the Greyville racetrack called Johnny Phedides, who was a great and well known character in Durban. He jumped into my father's arms when he saw him, as they had been cellmates all those years before. My father was very handy with a sewing machine and had made men's handkerchiefs in jail. Johnny could not sew and as a result my father would sew his 40 handkerchiefs a day, in exchange for a constant supply of cigarettes. My father got out of jail a couple of months before Johnny was supposed to come out and he asked my dad to please go and visit his dying mother. This my father duly did and also told her that Johnny was doing well and coming out soon. She unfortunately died before seeing her son again. He always kept his promises and was a very loyal friend. One thing about my father I would like people to know is that there were no grey areas in his life. It was black or white... Nothing in between. I think that must have rubbed off on me as well. His overall approach to life was something I always admired and I'd like to think that I inherited most of his traits.

His love of golf never waned and he eventually became a weekend golf pro at the Virginia Farm Golf Club, Johannesburg, in 1947. He was, by all accounts, an excellent coach who eventually went on to train more Springboks (as those who were chosen to play for South Africa were called at the time) than any coach before or since. In addition, he won many tournaments as well as sharing his love of the game with my mother, who, under his guidance, notched up a couple of wins in local tournaments.

We eventually lived on the golf course property and it was then that my interest in golf started. I'd like to say that I watched those my father coached and made a conscious decision to take up the game simply because I liked what I saw. This, however, was not the case and basically, I can lay the blame for my subsequent passion for golf firmly on the shoulders of my sister and the man who went on to become her husband.

Chapter Two

MY FRIEND, MY CONFIDANT, MY BROTHER-IN-LAW

I 'LL NEVER forget the first time I met the man who was destined to become my brother-in-law. I was a sociable kid and was always on the lookout for new playmates. Obviously, when I saw two boys kicking a rugby ball around on a grassy section next to the golf course I wanted to join in the fun and promptly asked if I could join the game. They weren't very impressed by an eleven year-old boy's attempts to butt in on their game and as such only allowed me to kick the ball a few times.

I thought the shorter of the two, a dark-haired boy, was called Gary Pal and only later found out that he was actually called Gary Player; the other chap was his step-brother, by the name of Christopher Goldsbury. Gary Player's father was having a game of golf with his good friend, Athol Rowen, who was one of the great cricketing brothers of South Africa at the time, and asked Gary to go and buy him a packet of tees from the pro shop. He walked in and saw my sister Vivienne who worked behind the till… It was love at first sight and so began my family's relationship with the man who would go on to become one of the most famous golfers in the world.

Gary had a profound effect on my life from the moment we met. I had always wanted a brother and he fitted the bill perfectly. Like I said, Gary and my sister hit it off from the start and he started to spend every weekend at the golf course. It wasn't long before my dad started to give him lessons and although he struggled with his game in the beginning, his determination to master the game shone through and he improved at a dramatic rate.

My sister married Gary in January 1957, four years after he had turned professional. He had made a deal with my sister saying that he would marry her if he won the Ampol Tournament in Melbourne Australia. The prize money was fantastic at the time and in addition to marrying my sister, he promised to buy me a white sports coat. He took the title – my sister got a wedding ring and I got the coat.

Like so many sporting wives before her, my sister gave up an enormous amount when she married Gary. When she got married she was playing off a scratch handicap and had been chosen to represent South Africa as a Springbok. At that time, Gary, who was playing in the US, phoned her to say he was feeling lonely and she must join him. She essentially gave it all up, choosing instead to travel the world with her up-and-coming sports-star husband.

One of the things that has irked me throughout my career as a golfer was the fact that just about everyone referred to me as Gary Player's brother-in-law – the fact that I was Bobby Verwey meant very little. No matter how well I played or which tournaments I won, the headlines, particularly in South African publications, simply had to mention the fact that I was related to Gary. Everyone wants their fifteen minutes of fame; however, in my case, every time I won a title or played well, I was forced to share that with my incredibly famous brother-in-law. It was, at times, a bitter pill to swallow.

Don't get me wrong – I have never been jealous of Gary and we enjoyed a very close bond when we were growing up. We may have both been passionate about the game of golf, but our opinions have always differed on what we wanted to get out of the game. The one thing I have always admired about Gary are his impeccable manners both on and off the golf course. He always dressed immaculately and he has a memory like an elephant – he never forgot a face or a name. Gary is also a speaker of note and has always made South Africa proud.

Gary's mother died from cancer when he was eight years old and although he always claimed to come from a very poor family (his father worked on the gold mines) he went to the best schools and always wore good clothes. His father, 'Whiskey' Player, remarried later in life to a lady called Dorothy Goldsbury, who hailed from Rhodesia (now Zimbabwe) and had two children of her own. The story goes that none of the Player children were happy with this arrangement and Gary's brother, the late Ian Player, a famous wildlife conservationist, dropped out of school and joined the army, while Wilma, Gary's beautiful sister, accepted the first decent marriage proposal that came along and Gary – then aged 16 – came to live with us.

We shared a bedroom for three or four years and would spent hours talking about our hopes and dreams and sharing our secrets – boy, if those walls could talk! He used to tell me how he was going to become the best golfer in the world and how his father had named him after the actor Gary Cooper, who had acted in *High Noon*. Gary adored Western movies and stated that he wanted to wear black because all the baddies wore black. He was determined to portray, as much to himself, as to the world, that he was a mean machine – someone who had a killer instinct and who would stop at nothing to be the very best. I hung on to every word – why wouldn't I? Gary had become my idol, a sort of big brother that I looked up to and loved.

In my opinion, Gary was often too hard on himself, I remember well the first time he entered the South African Open which was held at the Zwartkops Country Club in Pretoria. Although, there was a field of less than a hundred players, he failed to make the cut. That night, when we sat down to eat, he was nowhere to be seen. It turned out that he was outside in tears about his loss. When my father heard about this, he tore outside and gave him a seriously good man to man talk (and a couple of smacks), telling him that if he wanted to marry his daughter, he had to man up, and had better practise a lot harder. It seems that Gary took his advice because he went on to win the tournament the following year.

Gary now owns a very successful stud farm in Coles-berg, South Africa, which has bred some outstand-ing racehorses, and I would like to think that his love for these animals came from the years that we spent together when growing up. I had owned my own horse since the age of eleven. One day, my father went to an auction to buy a cow to supply the clubhouse and farm with milk. He may have gone off with this intention, but instead he bought a horse that caught his fancy. He managed to pay someone who rode the horse bare-back, all the way from Bree Street in Johannesburg – a distance of around 35 kilometres (about 22 miles), while my dad followed in his car. When he picked me up from school that day, he jokingly told me that he'd bought me a 'donkey'. Needless to say, I fell in love with my little chestnut mare named Judy and rode her every day. Gary also rode her on occasion and darn well nearly broke his neck in the process. One day, while galloping Judy on the fairway, he took a tumble and came crawling back to the clubhouse on his hands and knees and I had to go and find Judy as Gary was hurting all over and unable to walk.

It would be fair to say that the only reason I took up golf at the grand old age of 11 was so I could tag along with Gary and my sister. As I showed a bit of interest, my father started coaching me and it was immediately apparent that I had been blessed with a natural talent for the sport. I never had a very good golf swing, but I always had an incredible ability to score well – some-thing that stood me in good stead throughout my career.

Although my father was a phenomenal coach and renowned for getting a person playing a good game within a short amount of time, for some reason, he never really focused on my swing. I don't know why and I certainly don't hold it against him. Of course, my large size was always going to be against me, but it has to be said that the overall standard of coaching wasn't that high during this time and I do believe that I would have had far more success had I worked with someone that focused on every aspect of my game. Unfortunately, by the time it became apparent that my swing needed attention, the coaches I did approach weren't that keen to take me on. At the age of 19 or 20, I think they thought that it would be a case of trying to teach an old dog new tricks and I was basically left to my own devices.

I entered my first amateur tournament when I was 11 years old, when my father received special permission for me to enter the Royal Johannesburg Junior Golf Championship, which was traditionally reserved for kids aged between 12 and 15 years. As luck would have it, I had to play against the oldest boy taking part, who also happened to be twice my size. I'll never forget his name, Roland Rex, and that he hailed from the mining town of Springs, east of Johannesburg. He had only just started playing golf too and like me was still wet behind the ears as far as the rules were concerned. I lost the first six holes and on the seventh green had to putt for about a metre for a five. Roland, who was out of bounds on that hole had a half metre putt for a seven. In effect, I could two putt to win the hole. The first putt landed two centimetres short so I confidently walked up and tapped the ball into the hole. Unbeknown to me, the rules dictated that the person whose ball was furthest from the hole putted first. My father walked up and made Rex claim the hole from me, something he was extremely reluctant to do. Now instead of being five down, I ended up being seven down. I cried all the way to the next hole because I truly believed that I had won that hole fair and square. I went on to halve that hole, but lost both the ninth and eighth hole. I did, however, learn a valuable lesson that day – the person whose ball is furthest from the hole plays first.

I was a tall child, measuring 5'9" and weighing somewhere in the region of 80 kilogrammes (around 176 pounds) by the time I was 13. If there is one sport that South Africans are passionate about, it's rugby and although I never took to the game with quite as much gusto as golf, I was considered a reasonably good player. I also enjoyed the odd game of cricket, managing to make it onto the second eleven team. My sister, Vivienne, also sporty, started swimming, training with a top-notch South African swimming coach at the time, Cecil Colwyn, and later went on to become the SA Junior Backstroke champion. I used to spend hours at the pool with her and as such became a very competent swimmer.

Although rugby, swimming and cricket kept me pretty busy, golf was the sport where I really excelled. By the age of 13, I stood out as a very good golfer. I won my first Junior championship that year by 22 strokes. Named the Prentice Memorial Trophy, I won it 30 years after my father had taken the same title. My amateur golfing career really started to take off from this point and I never lost a Junior championship game before I turned pro at the age of 18.

Between the ages of 15 and 17 my game reached a new high and I won a large number of amateur golf tournaments, including the Transvaal Amateur Championship, the Vaal Amateur Championship, East Rand Amateur Championship, Western Transvaal Amateur Championship and the Natal Amateur Championship. At that stage, amateur golf was incredibly strong and featured players such as Reg Taylor, Dennis Hutchinson, Arthur Walker, Arthur Stewart, Allan Jackson, Bob Williams, Vernon Beuthin, Ian Head, and Rodger Brewes, to name a few.

I had a scratch handicap by the time I was 14. I was spending every available spare minute on the golf course by that stage and I knew that I was going to become a professional golfer. My determination to crack the game started playing havoc with my schooling and I clearly remember my French teacher, a Mr Van der Vyfer, telling me that I was never going to amount to anything. A couple of years after I left school, I was driving in my fancy new car when I spotted him walking down the road. I stopped and offered him a lift – of course, my kind offer was refused and he stomped off, muttering unintelligible words under his breath. Fortunately, the headmaster, a Mr Bovat, was an avid golf fan and would always give me permission to take off school to play. Needless to say, I always managed to score A's in most of my subjects – unfortunately, in my case, the A's stood for 'absent'.

I left school at 17 and found work at the Ocean Fish Supply in Johannesburg. My job involved weighing fish and making up orders for local shops and hotels in the area. The job, while fairly enjoyable, did have a major drawback – the smell. I worked there for a year and can categorically state that it takes roughly three days to get the smell of fish off your hands. I was paid the princely sum of R70 (roughly $5.80 in today's terms) a month and got to work and back on a scooter, although it needs to be noted that I didn't bother with the small things in life such as getting a licence!

The owner and my boss, Max Greenstone, was himself a keen golfer and had promised to support my career goals and sponsor me once I had turned pro. I will forever remain in his debt for his belief in me. I went on to befriend his son David, who not only became my best friend, but was the best man at my wedding. We played a lot of golf together: when I first met him he was playing off a 22 handicap, and a year later he was playing off scratch. We played a lot of friendly matches against other golfers, making lots of money when we invariably won. In addition to being an excellent golfer, David was also an avid exponent of Karate karateka and went on to earn his Springbok colours in that sport.

Chapter Three

BEING AN AMATEUR AND NOT A SPRINGBOK

I TOOK part in my first amateur international tournament in 1958 and interestingly enough, got my first taste of what it felt like to live the high life. My father had been giving golfing lessons to a certain Mr Peavy, a director of the Bell Telephone Company in London, and mentioned that I would be coming across to the UK. Mr Peavy told him to send him the details of when I was arriving and the flight number as he would send someone to pick me up from the airport and show me around London. When I landed, a chauffeur in a big, black Bentley met me and proceeded to check me in at the Savoy Hotel with instructions to order what I wanted to eat and drink and charge it to Mr Peavy's account. I had been pretty impressed by the little bit of London that I'd seen driving from the airport, although nothing could have prepared me for what I found in the room once I'd booked in – television. There was no such thing in South Africa at the time (TV was only introduced in the mid-'70s) and I proceeded to sit and watch everything on offer (including the British national anthem) until the programming ended at 10pm. I think I have to have gone down as the cheapest, happiest guest the Savoy ever had the pleasure of hosting – and although I could have ordered anything off the menu, I settled for a grilled sandwich and a Coca-Cola. The next morning the chauffeur took me to see all the sights of London before I was taken to my accommodation in Sunningdale where I was paying the grand sum of 75 cents a night. Driving past the small, grey houses I couldn't help but wonder if this was the first time that the residents had ever seen a Bentley passing through their neighbourhood.

When I knocked on the door, the landlady informed me that she had another golfer staying there, a certain Bob Charles from New Zealand. Bob and I became great friends. At 22 he was tall, dark and somewhat handsome. He had been a bank teller in New Zealand and had won a number of amateur local tournaments before coming across to Britain to see how his game would compare to other amateurs in Europe. Although he was right-handed, he became the first golfer to win tournaments playing a left-handed game. We ended up travelling around Britain in a navy blue Austin that the late, great Australian golfer Norman von Nida lent us. Norman was known as quite a character. He was small in stature, bad-tempered and a big-time gambler. One of his more famous quotes was: 'I made more money playing golf with the bookies and betting on the horses than from golf.'

A number of years after he left the circuit, he wrote a book called *Golf Was My Business* and one of the stories relates to an incident with the brilliant American golfer Walter Hagen, who played a lot of exhibition matches around Australia. Norman, who never lacked in confidence approached Walter and said, 'Mr Hagen, I would like to be your caddy... ' Walter responded by saying, 'Son, you do know that I am the best golfer in the world?'

Norman, who was never at a loss for words, replied, 'Sir, you do know that I'm the best caddy in the world?'

Hagen promptly replied, 'Well then I think we'll make a great team.'

Norman went on to caddy for the great man, adding another couple of wins to his belt in the process.

Although Bob and I travelled around England together and it was great to have a golfing companion, nothing prepared me for my first visit to Scotland to play at St Andrews. To coin a British phase, it bucketed down for the entire trip. It was cold, I was soaked to the skin and perhaps for the first time since I'd left, I missed my mother and the comforts of home. I don't know if this impacted on my game (I was knocked out in the quarter finals), but I can tell you that I didn't enjoy playing at St Andrews initially. It's one of those courses that needs to be mastered and understood and it took me some years and a lot of playing before I eventually grew to love this world-famous course.

Bob and I became closer on and off the fairways and we spoke about a lot of things and one night we both confessed that we were virgins. We both decided that it was time to rectify this particular situation and agreed that plans would be made when we got back to Sunning-dale. A couple of days after our return we caught the train to London and made our way to Soho where we came across two very tall, large-breasted prostitutes on a street corner. Sheepishly, we asked how much it was and were told it was 30 shillings each. So upstairs we went, but all too quickly, in just a matter of minutes, I was down the stairs again and to my surprise found Bob waiting for me. We took the train back to Sunningdale. Strangely, neither of us discussed on the train, what happened, but when we got back to the room, Bob, convinced that he was going to catch some dreadful disease simply by being in such a place, removed all his clothes and chucked them into a basin of scalding hot water.

We used to play Blackjack in our room on quiet days and he always insisted on being the banker. We played for a couple of cents and pennies and he was always quick to remind me the next day if I owed him a cent or two. I usually paid my gambling debts very quickly before he started reminding me all over again. Inter-estingly, enough we met years later in 2004 and took a bet for £100 as to the All Blacks Rugby team beating the South African Springboks at Ellis Park. Both New Zealanders and South Africans are very passionate about rugby and feelings generally run high when these two particular teams face off. To my absolute delight the Springboks annihilated the All Blacks on this particular occasion, beating them 40-26. I'm not sure if Bob has forgotten, but he still owes me that £100.

When Bob came to South Africa to play in the World Amateur Championships in Johannesburg, I introduced him to my sister's best friend, Verity Aldridge and they married a few years later. Bob of course has gone on to great things and is now known as Sir Bob Charles.

Although by all accounts it has been a long and happy marriage, Verity used to tell me how Bob drove her crazy with his obsessive cleanliness. Apparently, he used to get up hours before a tournament and press his trousers, press his shirt and iron his socks as well as his underpants. He used to also clean his shoes over and over again. Everything, down to his hat and golf clubs, was always meticulously clean and perfect. Years later, he won the British Open in the same year that I took the Senior British Open title, where he was the runner-up to me.

I eventually left Britain and competed in the European Amateur Tour for around three months. While I obviously remember the great golf, I also remember the rain and boy, did it rain while I was there!

There were many highlights, but one of the most amazing things I can remember happened on a golf course in Paris. I'd gone to the St Germaine golf course for a practice round. Amateurs apparently didn't warrant caddies and I was pulling my own trolley with my clubs. As I walked to the tee, an elderly couple asked if they could walk the nine holes with me. Hungry for company I said that it would be lovely and that they were welcome to join me. I took my driver and ball, hit my driver off the first tee, looked up and saw the gentleman pulling my trolley. I protested, but he said he was more than happy to help and when we got to the green he handed me my putter and held the pin. He continued doing this for the next nine holes. After I'd finished they took me to the clubhouse and bought me a Coca-Cola. Shortly after they had left, the tournament director approached me and smilingly said that I surely mixed in high class circles these days. I was more than a little confused and asked what on earth he was on about. It turned out that the elderly couple were Prince Edward, Duke of Windsor, formerly known as King Edward VIII and his wife Wallis, the Duchess of Windsor. The man who had given up the British throne for the woman he loved had kindly kept me company and had acted as a caddy to a naive 17 year-old South African kid. To put it mildly, I was gobsmacked and felt incredibly honoured!

Another highlight occurred while at the Royal Birkdale Golf Course which is situated in Southport, near Blackpool. I was playing with a chap called Charles Laurie, who I believe went on to become heavily involved with, among other things, the redesign of the golf course at St Andrews. I'd been playing well, but it was only when I got to the last hole that Charles pointed out that I only needed to make a three on the last hole in order to break the course's all-time amateur record – he promised to buy me a bottle of champagne if I made the cut. I hit the ball around 40 feet from the pin and proceeded to sink the ball with the next putt. I didn't drink in those days and spent the next three hours in the company of one of golf's finest gentlemen drinking copious amounts of Coca-Cola.

Looking back, I now know that I turned pro just at the right time. However, deciding to leave my amateur status behind wasn't something that dominated my thoughts at the time. I wanted to play for South Africa, as a Springbok and take part in the Commonwealth Golf World Championships that were being played in Johannesburg. I was invited to take part in the trials. At that stage, I was on top form and everyone assumed that it was a certainty that I would make the team. I played in the trials and finished second. However, when it came to choosing the team, I was not chosen to play; in fact, I didn't even make it as a reserve. I can remember walking down the fairway sobbing. Here I was, one of the top two players in the country and I had been left out in the cold.

The selectors came up with all sorts of excuses as to why I had been excluded, including the fact that as I wasn't yet 18 years of age, I wouldn't be able to mix with the other players in the bar because I wasn't old enough to drink. The decision was slated by the South African media who noted that the South African Golfing Union should not have invited me to play in the trials if that was the case. More importantly, prior to all of this, I had just returned from my first European trip as an amateur where I had played some really good golf. I had won the German Amateur Championship, I was also the leading amateur in the French Open, played well at the British Amateur Championship, making it through to the quarter finals, and had qualified as the youngest player to ever qualify for the British Open. I was devastated: it seemed that no matter how well I did on the circuit,

I didn't qualify to become a Springbok. I turned pro the next day.

Chapter Four

TURNING PRO

I TURNED pro just before my eighteenth birthday and played my first professional tournament at Zwartskop Country Club, which was then the venue of the Northern Transvaal Championship. I lost, by one stroke, to a very fine player called Eric Moore and tied with Otway Hayes (Dale Hayes' father) and the great Bobby Locke. After this I was dubbed 'the new Bobby Locke' in newspaper reports and it followed me around for some time.

After the pro tour in SA, which finished in February 1960 and was sponsored by Max Greenstone, I was off to America. My amateur record was so good at this time that I was given an amateur tour card.

I was very, very excited by the time I arrived at my first tournament in Sarasota. I had been reading about the famous American players for years and was thrilled by the idea that I was going to get to meet and play with some of the all-time greats. The course was long and proved to be very difficult, which wasn't helped by the fact that I was in awe of the professionals taking part: needless to say, I didn't make the cut.

The next tournament was at the Azalea Open in Wormington, North Carolina where I missed the cut by only one shot. I was extremely disappointed, as I was now starting to find my game and my way.

After that I played in the Greensborough Open at the Starmount Golf and Country Club where I met Sam Snead who, in my humble opinion, remains one of the greatest golfers of all time. Things had started to come together and I played the last round with Ernie Borris, who was the brother of another exceptional player called Julius Borris. The reason this particular game stands out in my mind is that on the seventh hole after we drove off, I inadvertently played his ball. This meant an automatic two shot penalty. I finished in 35th place, winning the grand sum of $60 – definitely nothing in comparison to the gigantic prize money being thrown around by sponsors today.

I also played with Arnold Palmer in the Canadian Open. During the game he went for a par five across a very wide river. He hit a poor shot, which ended up on a small island in the middle of the river. The water was quite deep, and he had no apparent way to get there, he however, got a piggy-back ride from his caddy and hit the ball from the island. Although not cheating, he definitely took advantage of some of the rules.

What happened next had a great bearing on my career, 33 years later. Both Eric Brown, the famous Scottish golfer, and Leopold da Luiz needed a par to tie for the last hole and both drove into the bunker on the left side of the fairway. They each tried to reach the green from the bunker, but never got out of the bunker.

As a result, they both made sixes and lost their chance to win the British Open. I vowed that if was I ever in that position, I would try and get out of the bunker first and then take my chances from there.

The next tournament was the New Orleans Open. The reason I mention this specific event was because of a very unusual incident. For people who don't know, during the first two rounds, some tournament winners are paired. For example, players who have won a lot of money will play together, guys who have won a few tournaments will be teamed up and those who have won very little or no money will be paired. After two rounds, the pairings change and are made according to the individual's scores. They take them in blocks of six. One, three and five play together; two, four and six play together. It so happened that coming into the final round, only three South Africans were competing in the tournament. As a result, all three South African players were paired to play that round together: Gary Player, Harold Henning and I walked out to the first tee.

On the fifth hole – a par five – I was on the left side of the fairway, and in the process of playing my shot, my club hit a branch and I missed the ball completely. When I looked up Gary and Harold were rolling around on the fairway in fits of laughter. After nine holes I was out in 39 strokes and Gary and Harold in 34. I was complaining like mad while my two rivals tried to encourage me as best they could. After the ninth hole I started making a lot of birdies. By the time we got to the 17th tee, I was only two strokes behind the two of them.

At this stage they were still encouraging me. However, on the 17th green I sank a 25 footer for a birdie and when we walked to the 18th green, the calls of encouragement abruptly ceased – I was only one stroke behind. There were no more calls of encouragement after that. I hit a very bad drive on the 18th hole and had to chip back on the fairway after landing in the trees. It was a par five and both Gary and Harold were in the bunker for two strokes. I hit a six iron a foot from the pin, while Gary and Harold both made par which got us all in a tie for seventh place.

Following this, we played in the Oklahoma City Open... Strangely enough I played yet again with another South African, Dennis Hutchinson, as well as Bill Blanton, an American. Bill was a very long hitter. By the end Dennis and I both had played brilliantly and shot 65s, while Bill, who outdrove us seventy-five metres on each hole, had scored only a 76. He quit the tour straight after, never to play again. Dennis and I tied for fifth place.

The biggest tournament of 1960 was the Speedway 500 Festival. This $50,000 tournament, which was being played for the first time, coincided with the famous Indy 500 race on Memorial Day. We played on the Thursday, Friday, Saturday and then everyone went to the race on Sunday; we then finished the tournament on the Monday. In those days the course had nine holes inside the track and nine holes outside the track, which were linked by a subway or two. The first winner of this tournament was Doug Ford, who received $9,000.

The Indy drew thousands of spectators and as a result accommodation was very hard to come by. The tournament organisers had asked all us single guys to make use of private accommodation that was on offer. I had the honour of staying with a Mr and Mrs Bob Crouch who went on to became part of my extended family. For the next 55 years their home became my home-away-from-home. They weren't wealthy people, but that didn't stop them from building a room onto their house and opening their doors. Whenever I played in the US Often and had some time off, I would drive or fly to Indianapolis to enjoy some good home cooking and to spend time with my wonderful friends. Mrs Crouch died in 2013, but Mr Crouch – or Pappy, as I fondly call him – turned 96 in November 2014. He is like a second father to me and I have spent many an hour avidly listening to the stories about his life. He was in the US Navy and survived the attack on Pearl Harbor. A scratch handicap golfer himself, he always managed to get me the use of the Highland Country Club course every time I visited.

I didn't actually get to watch the Indy 500 until 1964. On that Sunday I went down to the race track and watched the race from the pits. On the second lap veteran driver Eddie Sachs and rookie A. J. McDonald crashed and both drivers died in a horrific fireball.

This was the first time in the history of the event that the race had been stopped for an accident. As a result of this incident, the use of gasoline in the race cars at Indianapolis was banned from 1965 onwards. That was my first experience of the Indianapolis 500 and I saw it many times after that in the years to come – although it has to be said that none of the other races I watched ever ended in such tragic circumstances.

Chapter Five

MAKING THE CUT

I RETURNED to Europe and it was there where I won my first professional tournament – the German Open Championship, which was played in Hamburg in 1961. It was particularly exciting because I managed to beat a Welsh player by the name of Brian Hugget by one shot on the 18th hole.

Shortly after this the German airline, Lufthansa, offered me free flights for a couple of years if I agreed to continue playing in the German Open. I was over the moon, as travel formed a big part of my expenses. During a conversation with, David Makepeace, the manager of Gary Player, I casually mentioned my exciting windfall. I received a call from the airline two days later to tell me that the offer was withdrawn. Needless to say, Gary Player received this contract, I learnt my lesson and tried to keep any future windfalls to myself after that.

My next and last tournament of that year was the 1960 US Open. It was a very tough tournament to qualify for – you have local qualifiers, sectional qualifiers and more than five thousand other players in contention before you even got to the US Open. After being successful in both the local and sectional qualifying stages I made it into tournament, which was played at Cherry Hills Country Club in Denver, Colorado.

That particular year there were 3,800 entries for the few available spots and the first qualifier took place at Greenbriar in West Virginia. I managed to make it through and turned my attention to the next stage, which meant that I had to get to St James River Golf Club in Richmond, Virginia, by the very next day. I eventually ended up hitching a ride with Ansel Snow, another entrant, we drove for seven hours through the mountains before arriving at the club at around 5.30am. We managed to wake up a security guard who helpfully let us in and found someone to cook us up a breakfast. At that stage there were 37 players playing for three places. I remember scoring 74 and 71 and finishing in a tie with two others for the third spot. Unfortunately, one of the other players in the sudden death playoff happened to be Ansel. I had a seven-metre putt and I just knew that I was going to sink the ball and get the spot, essentially beating the man who had gotten me to the qualifier in the first place.

Three weeks later, it was time for the sectional qualifier, which was taking place at the Twin Hills Country Club in Oklahoma City. At this stage there were 65 players vying for 12 places. These were all good players and were all part of the tour. I played really well until the last hole. I chipped out about 50m in two shots where I proceeded to shank my pitch out of bounds. I proceeded to hit the next on to the green for six, but I knew that I had blown my chances of securing a spot and was feeling pretty down. You can only imagine my elation when one of the officials told me that the US Golf Association had changed the rules that year and that an out of bound shot only counted off a shot and not playing off the tee. I had to wait a couple of hours to see if I'd performed well enough, but at least I was in with a chance. It turned out that there were six of us who were tied for the last two places. I used the time wisely and rushed to the practice tee... and proceeded to hit 10 perfect shanks in a row.

Jackie Burke Jnr, Millar Barber, Jerry Pitman, Lenny Woodward, Jack Ellis and I were all vying for two spots. Barber, Pitman and Burke all bogeyed the hole. Woodward, Ellis and I went to the second hole where we all parred and proceeded to the third hole. I hit a good drive and a wedge for my second shot. My knees were shaking – I'd just shanked 10 balls and wasn't feeling confident at all. However, my powers of concentration kicked in and I managed to hit the ball seven inches from the hole – made the birdie and secured my spot in the Open.

The rest of the guys went to the eighth hole having halved every preceding hole – it was turning out to be a fight to the death, until a PGA official came over and told them to pick up their balls – they were both in the US Open. As it turned out, another player, Charlie Coe, had enjoyed a couple of drinks to celebrate his US Open qualifier, then went to shower and unfortunately had slipped and broken his leg.

When I got to Denver, I discovered that Ben Hogan, Sam Snead and Jack Nicklaus, who was still an amateur at that stage, had all made the cut.

I was feeling great. Here I was, a 19 year-old South African, who had made it through to one of the greatest tournaments in the world – yep, I was young, I was fit and healthy and I was playing well – what could possibly go wrong? The answer... unfortunately, came rather quickly. One of the side-effects of extensive long-haul travel is haemorrhoids. I'd never experienced anything like it. I was playing a practice round with Stan Leonard when my butt began to really hurt, I was in agony and was promptly dispatched to the clubhouse where they immediately sent me off to a local doctor. Fortunately for me, he saw me immediately, gave me an injection and whipped the offending protrusion off, reassuring me that I'd be right as rain in the morning. He was right: I played a perfect practice round the next day.

The tournament started and I played well, scoring 75 and 72 on the first day. By the time I got to the final hole on the second day, I was two under par for that round and needed a par for 70, which would enable me to make the cut quite comfortably. The 18th must be one of the toughest par four holes I personally have ever played. You drive over water and out of bounds on the rough elevated green: I promptly hit my drive out of bounds and proceeded to hit the next shot straight into the rough before eventually hitting the ball short on the green. I had chipped the ball about four metres past the pin when friends who had come to watch me play informed me that I had to sink that putt in order to make the cut. I missed it by four metres and knowing that I was out of the tournament, I casually walked up to the ball and putted it in to the hole for what I thought was a seven which gave me an overall score of 73, which meant that I had missed the cut by one stroke. With a heavy heart, I sat at the marking table with my playing partner, Johnny Pott who went through my score card. He was adamant that I had scored 72, but despondently, I told him he was wrong and that my calculations were correct. He refused to listen and carefully studied the score I'd recorded for each hole. He insisted that I'd scored a six on the last hole, pointing out that thanks to the new law regarding out of bounds shots, the one shot hadn't counted at all. Once again I was saved by the new ruling – I had made the cut and had made it into the top 50 which allowed me to carry on playing for the next two days in the final two rounds.

It turned out to be an incredibly exciting tournament. Arnold Palmer had started five shots behind the leader, but had birdied the first six holes and eventually went on to win the title – however, not before various dramas were played out by other contenders.

Ben Hogan had had a chance for a win. However, on the 17th hole his third shot hit the pin and went into the water; Jack Nicklaus went on to secure second place to Arnold. Tommy Bolt was also in with a chance until he hit his drive into the lake on the last hole. Renowned for his temper, he promptly hurled his driver into the lake and stomped off in a rage. The lake was only two or three feet deep and the club landed in such a way that the grip sank into the mud, leaving the head of the golf club sticking out. His caddy had asked if he should retrieve the club for him, but Tommy, swearing and cursing, said (amongst other things) no. He proceeded to walk away, then turning around suddenly saw that a young boy was wading into the lake in order to get the abandoned golf club. Tommy screamed at the child, telling him to bring the club to him. The boy, however, was reluctant to hand over his hard-earned, somewhat ill-gotten gains, promptly gave Tommy the middle finger and ran off with Tommy in hot pursuit.

As for me, well I was very proud of my performance. I had played my personal best, made the cut, eventually tying in 40th place. I felt this was a great achievement for a 19 year-old and I was very happy with my lot.

Although I didn't know it at the time, my life was about to get even happier and more complicated as I started on the next chapter of my life – marriage and fatherhood.

Chapter Six

A MARRIED MAN

I MET my future wife a year after the US Open, when Gary and I went to visit a jeweller friend of his in Johannesburg. I was introduced to Nicolette – Nikki – Caras who was working as the jeweller's receptionist at the time. A runner up in the 1961 Miss Universe competition, she had been offered a contract with the Hollywood studio MGM, who not only coached her but also offered her a role in *Mutiny on the Bounty*. She led a very glamorous lifestyle in Los Angeles and mixed with famous personalities such as Frank Sinatra and Elvis Presley at the various house parties she attended. She was dubbed a Jean Simmons lookalike and was destined to become a great star. However, after about a year, she became disillusioned and unhappy and approached Sam Spiegel, one of the bigwigs with MGM at the time, and asked to be released from her contract. Marlene Dietrich was the first person to be released from a contract with MGM and Nikki was the second.

She eventually returned to South Africa and starred in a few Afrikaans movies before I met her. I was impressed with this gorgeous girl from the moment

I met her and really wanted to get to know her better. I phoned her that evening to ask her out, but she told me she already had a date. I was a charmer of note and managed to convince her to cancel and go out with me instead – which, much to my surprise, she did. We hit it off from the start and after a few short months got engaged. I was playing in the Sunshine Tournament in South Africa at the time, which took place between December and February. I'd performed well and had won the Western Province Open by six shots at the Royal Cape Golf Course. We got married at the beginning of March 1963, two days after my 23rd birthday, and went to Durban for our honeymoon where I took part in a tournament at the Durban Country Club – unsurprisingly, I missed the cut.

We both decided that I had to take part in the European Tour that year and although I played some of my best golf, finishing second, third or fourth, I never won a tournament. At the end of the season, I took a close look at my finances and was shocked to discover that although I had earned the accolade of being in the top six money earners, I had failed to turn a profit. I returned to South Africa and won the Transvaal Open Championship (I went on to win the same title five times during my career) at the Bryanston Country Club.

It was at this point, we decided it would be best for me to go back to the US and take part in the US Tour. I had a tour card and was eligible to work there. Sadly, despite the fact that European courses suited my style of play better and I had no doubt that I would have won a lot more tournaments, there was no way that I could survive on the lower prize money on offer – I, like everyone else, needed to earn a decent living.

One of the biggest benefits of joining the US Tour was the number of friends I made. At that stage the professional golfing community was very close knit and Nikki and I made friends with the likes of Arnold Palmer, Jack Nicklaus, Harold Henning, Jim Colbert, Bert Yancey, Dave Hill and Tony Jacklin, to name a few.

It wasn't all about golf and the fact that we always stayed at the same hotels while we were on tour meant that the wives of the various golfers also formed a bond. Looking back, I have to say that it couldn't have been easy for the wives whose husbands spent most days on the golf course. The players also spent a great deal of time together off the greens playing as much bridge as the wives would allow. Of course it wasn't long before the competition at the bridge table became as competitive as our tussles on the golf course. We all took the game very seriously and could lose as much as $30 in an evening. Yes, I know it doesn't sound like much, but believe you me, it was a small fortune at the time. To be honest we all became obsessed with the game and would whip out the cards at any given opportunity. I remember the following incident clearly.

We were taking part in a tournament in Dallas when it started to pour with rain and we were forced to go back to the hotel. We started playing bridge after lunch and I basically ignored Allan Henning, of the great Henning golfing family, when he walked in with some foreigner and I didn't pay much attention to the Italian man who took a seat behind me until he started making the odd comment about my hand, stating what I should and shouldn't have done. I'm not known for having a quick temper, but was slowly beginning to get hot under the collar. I ignored him flat and fortunately after a while he and Allan got up and left the room. The next day I asked Allan who the hell that irritating guy had been who had the cheek to tell me how to play bridge – only to be told that he was part of a group of Italian bridge players who were on tour in Dallas. Apparently they had been playing bridge for some 20 years and were called the Italian Blue Team. Internationally recognised, they represented Italy in international contract bridge tournaments and had won numerous world titles. To my embarrassment, the man who I thought had had the absolute audacity to give me a couple of tips obviously knew what he was talking about, as he was Carl'Alberto Perroux, the famous team's captain.

Although much of the goings-on off the golf course was harmless fun, not all of the golfers were squeaky clean. Nikki was an exceptionally attractive woman and had to endure being hit on by a number of golfers at the time. It was a long time ago so I'm sure they won't mind if I mention their names. Doug Saunders, Tommy Bolt, as well as a well-known married top golfer (I won't name and shame him), asked her out on dates. I suppose it was understandable – most of the guys played over-seas for extensive periods. They were lonely and in need of a bit of female companionship.

Another well-known married personality in golfing circles had a torrid affair with a very famous French lady for five or six years – to most of us it was common knowledge. Fortunately, due to the lack of media attention and the absence of the paparazzi in those days, they got away with far more than what was made public during the Tiger Woods scandal in later years. Nobody talked and most of us simply looked the other way, leaving most of the wives none the wiser.

I played in the Texas Open in San Antonio and was again very unlucky not to win. I finished two shots behind the winner, Arnold Palmer. Two years later a fellow South African and one of my best friends, Harold Henning, did win on this course.

At around the same time we played in the Sahara International in Las Vegas. We were staying in a small hotel on the Vegas Strip and I was fortunate enough to be driving a black Lincoln Continental on loan from Bob Charles. I shot a 66 on the first round and was two shots behind the leader, Dick Sykes. The third score was 68 or 69. I was sitting in a pretty good position. On the second day I was scheduled to tee off at eight o'clock. I asked the receptionist for a wake up call at six in order to give me enough time to get dressed, have breakfast and squeeze in a few practice shots. She informed me that they only opened at 7 o'clock and I would therefore have to set my own alarm. I went to bed late and somehow managed to set my alarm to the incorrect time. To my absolute horror I woke up at five minutes to eight. I leapt out of bed, grabbed my trousers, shirt and socks and proceeded to jump into the car wearing nothing but my boxers. I didn't have to worry about anything else as I knew my caddy would have my golf shoes and clubs waiting for me at the tee. I must have nearly broken the land speed record in the rush to get to the course and when I arrived in a cloud of dust, after initially missing the turn into the course, I left the car running and ran to the first tee, still in my boxers and still clutching my clothes. All of the other players and the tour director George Walsh were paralytic with laughter. The rule is, if you are late and the group in front of you has already played, you are automatically disqualified. If, however, you get there before they hit their second shot, you only receive a two shot penalty. Unfortunately for me, the players in front had just hit their second shot and were walking towards the green. Disqualified and feeling dreadfully sheepish, I returned to the car and got dressed while listening to the laughter still resonating off the fairway. When I got back to the hotel Nikki opened the door and started laughing at me and it was at that point that I too started to see the funny side of things. There was no point in crying over spilt milk, the damage had been done. We decided to make the best of a bad situation, we were in Vegas after all and went to the casino for the next two days – all was not lost and between us managed to win around $60. I learnt my lesson, though, and needless to say I received four or five alarm clocks for Christmas that year.

There were some real characters on the golf circuit in those years. Al Besselink (we called him Bessie), for example, was a very big gambler. One year he won a tournament, then went gambling where he lost everything in the casino and had to borrow money in order to get out of Vegas. An absolute charmer on and off the course, he collected quite a few millionaire wives in his lifetime. Unfortunately, they too had difficulty keeping up with his gambling.

Doug Sanders was another popular as well as a very colourful player. Dubbed by the press as the 'Peacock of the Fairways', he was certainly the best dressed player at the time, who traditionally never travelled with less than 20 pairs of shoes, trousers, with matching caps and shirts. One evening, as I was walking past the blackjack tables, he grabbed my arm and said that I must come and say hello to his girlfriend on the phone in London. I asked him who she was and he said her name was Jill St John. Not surprisingly, given the fact that she was a famous actress at the time, I recognised her name immediately. I can't for the life of me remember what I said to her during the call, but here's an interesting thing, I happened to bump into her years later when she was married to Robert Wagner and when I brought up that memorable phone call, she vehemently denied that she had ever dated Doug Saunders and speaking to me on the phone.

Another character worth mentioning, who also liked to gamble, was a Canadian, called George Knoetzen, one of the finest strikers of a golf ball that I have ever seen. A winner of a number of tournaments, he sadly died of cancer before his 50th birthday, just before starting on the Seniors Tour.

Chapter Seven

REFUSING A LUCRATIVE OFFER

A COUPLE of weeks after the Vegas incident, we were playing in the Waco Turner Open in Burneyville, Oklahoma. Waco Turner was an eccentric billionaire who had made his fortune in oil. He loved golf but hated sand traps, so when he built his own golf course, decided to leave them out completely. The tournament was played at the same time as the Tournament of Champions in Las Vegas. The golfers who played in the Waco Tournament were well paid for their efforts, receiving $15 for every birdie and $50 for every eagle and chip-in, regardless of the score. I had been playing very poor golf up until that point and was very low on funds. Actually, I was flat broke, having only enough money left to get to the tournament and was going to be in a whole heap of trouble if I didn't win. I dropped a shot to par the first hole, which was a long par four. I went on to par the second, fourth and fifth holes. On the sixth hole the players had to walk back about 150 yards to the tee while the caddies stood next to a stream slightly further up the course waiting for players to drive off. I hit my drive, the ball hit my caddy on the head and continued to bounce into the river. I made a triple bogey seven.

I was almost in tears by the time I got to the next tee, as it was clear that this was definitely going to be my last tournament in the US. My wife Nikki walked up to me and pointed out that at that stage things couldn't get any worse, they could only get better. Her words had a profound effect on my game and I proceeded to birdie most of the remaining holes, eventually shooting a 67 which put me tie for the lead. As things turned out, I finished third in the tournament behind a man by the name of Peter Brown, winning $1,700. This was an enormous sum back then and the win meant that I could continue on the circuit. My spirits were slightly dampened when I heard that the caddy I had inadvertently hit was attempting to sue me; however, in those days, these sort of cases were dealt with by the PGA, who I assume settled the matter – I certainly never heard any more about the lawsuit.

In those days the main sponsors of golf shoes was Foot Joy Footwear, closely followed by the Atonic brand. Our shirts were generally sponsored by Munsing Wear. It was extremely difficult to make a good living as a professional golfer back then, so, while I can fully understand that the sponsoring companies earned a great deal from using top golfers to market their products, it was, at the time, a win-win situation for both the players and manufacturers of golf wear.

It wasn't of course the only sponsorship on the table. I have Bob Charles to thank for being instrumental in securing a Dunlop sponsorship that saw me earning $4,000 a year to use their clubs and balls.

The next tournament I took part in was the Oklahoma City Open. On the Monday prior to this tournament I was invited to play in a charity Pro-Am at Southern Hills Country Club in Tulsa, Oklahoma. When I arrived on the Sunday evening, I heard that my amateur partner was Charlie Corly and he was keen to meet me before we teed off.

I was driving an old, beat-up Oldsmobile at the time and casually asked Charlie if he knew where I could get the car serviced. It turned out that I had the fortune of playing with the man who just so happened to own all the Oldsmobile dealerships in Tulsa and it wasn't long before one of his foremen arrived to collect the car.

The next morning, he picked Nikki and me up from the hotel and I proceeded to play an incredible round of golf, eventually scoring a 68. We won the tournament, which was no easy feat given that Southern Hills is regarded by most as being a very difficult course.

After the Pro-Am prize-giving, he took us back to his palatial home for dinner. He offered me a fantastic sponsorship which I had to really think very hard about. It was an awesome deal. I would receive a large sum of money for living expenses, enough money to play the tour in comfort, a free car as well as the offer to stay in his magnificent home during my spare time. In return, all he asked was for me to play golf with him and his friends for a month a year. With hindsight, I wish now that I had taken him up on his offer – he was a really great guy and it would probably have been a lot of fun hanging out with him and his friends. However, Nikki talked me out of it, mainly because she had great confidence in my ability to carry on and build my career.

In the morning when the foreman brought back my car, I was delighted to see that the car had four brand new tyres and a brand spanking new engine. The best news of all was that Charlie hadn't charged me a cent.

We then headed off to Oklahoma City to play in that tournament, where I had an incredible week. Indeed, if Arnold Palmer had not sunk a 45-foot putt on the 71st hole, I would not have finished second, but would have won the tournament.

Next we went to the Memphis Tournament, where I finished fourth on a golf course that I really enjoyed and loved and where I always played well. What was absolutely amazing is that all of this occurred a month after I was down to my last $10. In the space of a month I won in excess of $10,000 and was now driving a car that was virtually new. As they say in the classics, ' Fortune favours the brave'.

During the first two rounds of the tournament, I played with a golfing great, Tony Lema. Tony and I had become great friends; we had done a lot of carousing together before I got married. He was a character of note and a great guy. I wasn't aware that when he got married later, it was his second marriage and he already had a son called David, whom I am still in contact with today. After the second round, where Tony played exceptionally well, I remarked to Nikki that I couldn't believe that he wasn't a better player than his record showed.

However, a month or so later, after Nikki and I had returned to South Africa, I read that Tony had won his first tournament, and in the next six weeks went on to win four more. In my opinion he was, for the next two years, the best golfer in the world. He won the British Open and the Carling World Tournament, to name a few. On returning to the USA I played with him again in the fourth round at the Firestone Invitational in Akron, Ohio. As it happened neither of us played very well and he left to take part in an exhibition match in Idaho. Unfortunately, thanks to a pilot strike, most of the major airlines were grounded and he chose to charter a private plane to get from Akron to Chicago. Tragedy struck and the plane crashed on a golf course, killing both Tony and his wife, Betty.

After Memphis, Nikki went to spend two weeks with my sister, Vivienne, at her and Gary's home in the Bahamas. At the same time, I went to the UK to play in the British Open and the French Open. I played very, very well but putted poorly and lost to the great South American golfer Alberto de Vicenza. I returned to the USA where I took part in a number of tournaments before I met up with Nikki in Philadelphia and shortly thereafter, returned to South Africa, where I played the Sunshine Circuit.

Chapter Eight

FATHERHOOD

T HERE WASN'T much excitement in the first part of 1965; however, things did start heating up towards the end of that year when I returned to the States and started to play very well. I finished fourth in Portland, Oregon and seventh in another tournament that took place just outside Los Angeles. I won my first big US Tour event at the Almaden Open in San Jose, California. It was a fantastic feeling, not least because I thought the win would automatically open doors and get me into a lot of other top tournaments. At the very least, the win usually guaranteed a place in the Tournament of Champions and I naively thought that I would be invited to take part in the US Masters.

The invite never arrived. This came as a huge shock, considering that I had actually qualified for the event on two counts. I was very angry and hurt, as I was the first South African player to win a US Tour event and not get invited to the US Masters. I had also qualified on the basis of being one of the top two players in the fall tour. It wasn't the only thing that cut deep as, back in South Africa, my brother-in-law Gary Player's win in the

Australian Open covered virtually the entire back page of a major newspaper, while my bigger competition win only got a small mention at the bottom of the page.

Fortunately, the win did garner some respect in certain circles and when Nikki and I flew into Hawaii, where I was due to take part in the Hawaii Open, we were treated like royalty. We enjoyed a number of perks, like staying in one of the best hotels, which included the use of a chauffeur, who was on call 24 hours a day. It was magnificent. I'm not sure if the way I was treated relates in any way, but interestingly enough, Hawaii remains one of my all-time favourite places.

Unfortunately, our airline Pan American Airways had lost my golf clubs en route and I was forced to borrow clubs during the first round. However, It didn't seem to affect my performance and I shot a respectable 75 on the first day. The clubs were subsequently found and I proceeded to play even better, scoring 69, 69, 69, eventually finishing two shots behind the winners. I took fourth place simply because there were three players who had tied for first.

I left Hawaii in good spirits and returned to South Africa to wait for my invite to the US Masters. When the invite failed to arrive, I called Clifford Roberts, the man responsible for the invitations, but he refused to take my call. Although I had qualified, it has never been explained to me why I wasn't invited to the event and although I do have my suspicions as to why it happened, I don't have any proof.

Regardless of the reason, despite finishing in the top 20 for the next three years I failed to receive an invite.

The fact that I was overlooked still burns and I've often thought that I should have taken the matter further – who knows, with the right lawyer, the Augusta National Golf Course may have been called the Bobby Verwey Country Club!

We found out that Nikki was pregnant with our first child in September that year. Unfortunately, and much to my dismay, I was not able to be with her when our first son Robert Verwey Junior made his appearance in Pretoria, South Africa on 21 April 1966. I was on tour in the USA at the time, playing in the Tournament of Champions in Las Vegas. The best part of this competition was that just about everything was given to the players. Crocodile leather shoes and cashmere jackets, as well as a feast of entertainment, were part of the deal. I finished 10th out of a field of 25.

However, for once it wasn't golf that put me in the pound seats financially. Raymond Floyd introduced me to the game of Punto Banco and I enjoyed an incredible run of luck over the next three days. I won $15,000 in total, which was more than the tournament winner had pocketed. The win couldn't have come at a better time and I used the winnings to buy my first home in Randburg, South Africa.

The next tournament was in Flint, Michigan. This was a remarkable tournament, in the sense that I was known to be very short hitter and Warrick Hills where we played was one of the longest golf courses on the tour. I ended up finishing fourth and in addition to the prize money won the use of a new Buick for the next year. Needless to say, my golfing buddies who were golf pros, namely Harold Henning, Jim Colbert, Dave Eickle-berger and Dean Refrum, were suitably impressed.

We moved on to the US Open, which was being played at the Olympic Club in San Francisco. The venue is famously known as the place where Jack Fleck beat Ben Hogan a few years earlier – stopping Ben from winning his fifth US Open Title in a what had been a tremen-dously exciting competition. Although I managed to get my name on the leader board on a couple of occasions in the second and third rounds, I eventually finished 16th overall.

I returned to South Africa at the end of 1966 where I won a couple of tournaments, one being the Trans-vaal Open at Kensington and the other the Pepsi Cola Open, at Rand Park golf club. Married life was going well and Bobby Junior was growing up fast; however, there wasn't too much happening on the South African golfing scene at the time and we returned to the USA in March 1967.

It was a really good year for the wives as they all knew each other and the kids played together. They had their tea parties around the pool while we played golf. They would, on occasion, come to the golf course if one of the husbands played well and there was some prize-giving of sorts. Apart from Gary, Harold and me, there wasn't anyone else from South Africa on the US tour and it could have proved to be a lonely time for Nikki. The other players and their wives, however, went to great lengths to make us feel at home, including the likes of

George Arthur who arranged Bobby Junior's first birthday party.

We formed a really close bond, but the players whom Nikki and I were particularly close to included the likes of Harold Henning and his wife Patti, my sister Vivienne Player, Jim Colbert and his wife, Joe Archer, Jack Nicklaus, Arnold Palmer, Frank Beard and his wife Patti and Tony Jacklin and his first wife Vivienne. Vivienne Jacklin was an absolute honey, but sadly died a few years later from a brain aneurysm.

Speaking of close bonds, I've always been regarded as the joker of the family and as such wasn't averse to playing the odd practical joke on family members. One of the most memorable occurred when Larry Christie, a mechanic who had converted a 100-foot ex-MTB British warship into a fishing vessel, invited all the top South African golfers out for a day of fishing. Gary, who had never been on a boat before, was particularly nervous and wasn't very keen on the idea. However, he agreed to join us and as we boarded the rocking boat, he asked me whether the sea was going to be rougher than it was in the harbour. I jokingly told him, definitely not, pointing out that the sea was as calm as a lake. Of course, we started getting smacked around as soon as we left the safety of the harbour. I got seasick – hell, we all got seasick – however, Gary took this to a whole new level and literally turned green. He soon had his head deep inside a bucket. The crew were very understanding and periodically emptied and refilled the bucket to allow Gary to clean himself up, I found the whole thing a complete joke and started laughing. Unfortunately for me, Gary didn't see the funny side of things and promptly picked up the bucket filled with seawater and vomit and threw it all over me. Fortunately, for both of us, the boat hit a submerged log soon after and we had to return to port – with a very relieved Gary, no fish, and a slightly damaged boat, but not before I had made a promise to him that I would pay him back.

I bided my time, waiting for the perfect opportunity to come along and the next year we both played in the Greensborough Open and were staying at a Howard Johnson Motel. After playing golf we went back to the motel and dressed for dinner. We had a lovely meal at a nearby restaurant and when we returned to the motel, Gary, my sister Vivienne and a few friends were standing around admiring the beautifully lit pool. I noticed that Gary, who was immaculately dressed as always in white slacks, white shoes and a navy blue jacket and tie, was standing a little closer to the edge than the others. Coming up from behind, I reminded him of that disastrous day on the boat. He obviously knew what was coming and said that I would never dare to be that foolish. I ignored his protests and pushed him in. Everyone, except Gary, thought it was hilarious and while they cracked up with laughter, Gary, who was as mad as all hell, stomped off to get changed. I later heard that he had to put newspaper in his shoes and remove all the sopping wet money from his pockets and put it out to dry. When he returned I pointed out the reason and remarked: 'Paybacks are hard brother, paybacks are hard indeed.'

That year I decided to go and play in the British Open, at Royal Birkdale. My father was adamant that he wanted to caddy for me, which turned out to be quite an experience.

The funniest thing happened on the final round, on the fourteenth hole. It was a par three hole and I was driving into a very strong wind. My father wanted me to use a number two iron which would generally keep the ball low, but I wanted to use a number three wood. My father and I ended up having a full-on argument in full view of the spectators, because he refused to hand over the club I insisted on using. I eventually convinced him to hand over the preferred club, a three wood, and promptly hit a fantastic shot which landed an inch short of the hole. It so happened that there was a new Mercedes Benz up for grabs if you hit a hole in one. Highly indignant, my father told me that if I had used the two iron as he instructed, I would have made the hole and won the car. The whole thing must have seemed slightly bizarre to those who were watching; however, it was only when I saw my playing partner, George Archer, almost crying with laughter, that I was able to see the funny side of the situation.

You have to understand that prize money in those days was incredibly low and in no way compares to the enormous sums that the players earn today. To use an example: in 1962 when I won the German Open Championship, I won $300. Today the winner takes home in excess of $1 million.

Because the prize money was so low, you'd often find that players would play conservatively down the stretch.

We were all more focused on earning a good cheque instead of trying to go for an all-out win. So, in other words, while we all yearned to win, we tended to play on the safe side without much flair, in order not to mess our chances of earning some of the prize money.

It seems to me that I was very unlucky to end in a fourth or fifth position. I've always believed that good players make their own luck and on most tours where I was close behind the winner in second or third place, I lost because I didn't take advantage of the chances that I had to win the tournament.

Chapter Nine

CAREER DECISIONS

I RETURNED to South Africa in around September 1967, where I competed in the Sunshine Circuit. I lost to Cedric Amm in Durban at the Natal Open which took place at the famous Royal Durban Golf Club, in a 36-hole playoff where he scored 71, 71 to my 71, 72. The lead-up to the playoff was very tense and exciting. When I got to the 72nd hole, which was a par five, I needed an eagle to tie. It was downwind and I hit a good drive and then using a five iron hit the ball 20 feet past the hole. I then sank the putt and scored the eagle. All was not lost, however, and although I came second, I did manage to earn some extra cash during the tournament. It is incredibly hot and humid in Durban and for some strange reason the organisers decided that Cedric and I should both be paid the grand sum of R25 (approximately $2 in today's terms) for all our pain and suffering.

The following week, when I was in Cape Town, sitting on the veranda of Rondebosch Golf Club, I received a telegram from Nikki informing me that my invitation to the US Masters had finally arrived. I was over the moon, but, ironically, I wasn't playing very well at the time. We had also recently found out that Nikki was pregnant again and she wouldn't be able to join me at the tournament.

I have to say straight off the bat that the US Open is an incredible event. There's a distinct air of excitement and the buzz hits you from the moment you arrive. Disappointingly, I scored a 77 and 74 and missed the cut by a couple of shots. It's one of those tournaments where you have to actually take part in order to comprehend how difficult the greens are to putt on. Regardless, I did manage to win three bone china plates in the par 3 competition that was hosted before the main event. I was closest to the hole on all three, which I felt was quite an achievement considering that I was competing against 100 other players.

A heavily-pregnant Nikki eventually joined me in the States in June 1968. We travelled to Minneapolis, Minnesota in July, where I was competing in the Minnesota Golf Classic at the Hazeltine Golf and Country Club – which would go on to host the US Open two years later. At that stage, it was the longest golf course that anyone had played on during the US tour.

Everyone had complaints; the course was not only extremely long, it was also unbelievably difficult. I was told by numerous players that, as a short hitter, I would never finish. I proved them all wrong by making it through to the last round, playing with Bob Goldby – a former US Master's Champion – and Jay Herbert. To cut a long story short, I shot a 67 in the last round, which at the time was a course record by two shots.

Bob told me that it was the finest round of golf he had ever seen played – a huge compliment as he himself had played with the very best. Lew Graham, who went on to become a good friend, ended up beating me by one shot. It was the first tournament he had ever won and he later told me that had he been aware of my score he probably wouldn't have made it. As it happened, the course was relatively new and it was the first time a tournament had been held there. The scoreboards along the course had still to be erected and the fact that I was playing about four or five holes ahead of Lew meant that he remained blissfully unaware of my score and played an exceptional round, sinking a couple of long par shots. He went on to greater things and a few years later took the trophy at the US Open at the Madena Golf a Club in Chicago.

After that particular tournament, we travelled to Dallas, Texas and stayed with our best friends Bob and Verity Charles. It just so happened that Nikki and Verity were due to give birth at the same time and Bob and I took a few weeks off the tour to be with our wives and children. Bradley Jay Verwey was born on 25 August 1968; Bob's son, David, made his appearance the day after.

Bob and I really had our work cut out for us taking care of our older children who were both two years old at the time. However, the fun really started once the babies were born. In the USA, new mothers are generally discharged quickly after they have given birth and, true to form, Nikki and Verity were back home within a day of having Bradley and David. Neither she nor Verity were strong enough to look after the babies on their own, so Bob and I had to step in and do all the cooking and feeding for the two families. Before long, we had things down to a fine art: sometimes he would go to the store and buy food and other necessities, while I stayed at home and looked after the two newborns changing dirty diapers and cleaning dirty bums. Other times it would be up to me to do the shopping, leaving Bob to hold the fort while I was away.

If truth be told, it was a huge relief to get back on tour, we had never worked so hard and it actually felt like a bit of a holiday when we got back to playing golf. I think I can speak for Bob too when I say that to this day we both have an enormous amount of respect for mothers.

Years later, Bob's son David worked for the PGA of America and then became a big shot in the Senior Organisation. When I once missed out qualifying for the Senior PGA at the PGA National Golf club, West Palm Beach, I wrote him a nice letter. I asked him for a special invitation to this tournament and told him that I lost out by only one shot and would really appreciate it if he could put in a kind word for me. Sadly, I never received a reply.

Shortly afterwards, we once again returned to South Africa, I played in a few tournaments on the Sunshine Circuit, without much success. I did, however win two more tournaments, the Witbank Open and the Transkei Open in Umtata. Things remained quiet through 1969, but towards the end of that year I was offered a very good job at the Sandlefoot Cove Golf Club, Boca Raton, in Florida. We also found at that time that Nikki was pregnant again and I decided to take the job, mainly because I had a wife, two toddlers and a baby on the way.

The course was built by Bruce Devlin, an Australian pro and Bob von Hagge, a golf course architect who went on to build over 250 courses in 20 different counties around the world. On reflection, I quit playing on the US tour at the grand old age of 29 – far too early when you consider that most players are only starting their careers at that age.

I was the golf pro and the golf director and I became good friends with our two bosses, Howard Osterman and Jack Marquese. Jack was a real character, who had a voice very similar to the world famous French actor and singer Maurice Chevalier and used to entertain us all in the clubhouse. He had a terrific sense of humour, often noting that those who didn't like his voice couldn't kick him off the stage as he owned the joint.

Our third son Darren Kel Verwey was born on the 11th February 1970 in Fort Lauderdale, Florida. Despite regretting my decision to leave the US tour, I truthfully have to admit, I had a great few years at Sandlefoot and was paid really good money.

In 1971, while Bobby Jnr was attending a junior school in Boca Raton, I received some information that made me sit up and evaluate my life.

Dick Wilson and his wife who ran a newspaper in Deerfield Beach did a survey regarding drug abuse in American schools. At that stage, the statistics indicated that around 80 percent of school-going children under 10 years of age were either taking drugs or were in the company of children who were. The statistics were terrifying and we took the decision to return to South Africa, even though Jack offered me a lot more money to stay. With me it has always been a case of missing America when I was in South Africa and missing South Africa when I was in America. Before I left the USA, I had tendered and already bought the rights to the Golf shop at Windsor Park, in Durban.

Chapter Ten

TRUTH ALWAYS BETTER THAN FICTION

LOOKING BACK, some of the best years of my life were spent on the US tour. I played that circuit for nine years and made some incredible friends including Jack Nicklaus, Lee Trevino, Harold Henning, Tony Lehmer, Sam Snead, Doug Saunders, Jim Colbert, Bert Yancy and Tommy Aaron, and more. All became legends in their time and it was a privilege to not only know them, but to compete with them on the course.

Jack Nicklaus, for example, is one of the most generous and kindest men that I have ever met. He always seemed to go out of his way to be nice to me. At one stage he pulled me aside after a tournament to try and help with my swing. Unfortunately, as with most other champion players, his coaching abilities left a lot to be desired.

Friends aside, I also played some good golf and although I only had one win at the Almaden Tournament in San Jose in 1965, I racked up 42 top ten finishes.

Sadly, although I had managed to make a name for myself in the USA, I never really received the recognition from my fellow countryman in South Africa. In some way this was understandable – like I said earlier, South Africa didn't have television until the mid-1970s and although the larger tournaments were discussed in the local newspapers, overall very little attention was paid to most of the players who hailed from this part of the world.

South Africa had started to get the world's attention for all the wrong reasons during this period. Apartheid was in full swing and although I didn't necessary agree with the laws, as a South African I definitely bore the brunt of many of the country's decisions of that time.

The press, of course, didn't always get things right and one particular incident really got under my skin. Swesunker 'Papwa' Sewgolum was a self-taught South African golfer of Indian descent, renowned for his unorthodox way of holding a golf club (he played the game using a back-handed grip, now commonly referred to as the Swesunker grip). Born to a blind mother in extremely modest circumstances, he didn't attend school in his younger years, choosing instead to hit balls on the beach, using anything that resembled a golf club. The practice sessions obviously paid off and it quickly became clear that this was a player to be reckoned with. He won the Natal Amateur title at the tender age of 16. He later became a caddy at the Beachwood Country Club in Durban to make ends meet and it was here that he met a successful businessman by the name of Graham Wulff who recognised the youngster's talent and helped pave the way for Swesunker's future success. Swesunker went on to win the Dutch Open three times, in 1959, 1960 and 1964. In 1965 he returned to South Africa and defeated Harold Henning to win the Natal Open. The win made international headlines, although it has to be said that this wasn't only due to the fact that Papwa had taken the title.

In those days, the Apartheid laws dictated that a 'person of colour' was not allowed to frequent white establishments and, simply put, he was not allowed into the clubhouse to receive his trophy. Understandably, the press had a field day and basically tarred all of the South African players with the same Apartheid brush, stating that Swesunker had been forced to stand in the rain while the likes of myself and Dennis Hutchinson, who were the runners up, languished in the nice warm clubhouse. That wasn't the case at all.

They basically crucified us for something that was completely out of our control. Indeed, as the Captain of the PGA, I had lobbied hard in order for him to receive the same privileges as the other players. I'm not suggesting for a moment that we felt good about presenting an extremely talented golfer with his award outside in the rain; however, Nikki and I stood outside and were with him during the prize-giving. The press was so busy creating an uproar about this that they failed to mention that he was the first non-European to ever compete in an all-white sporting event in South Africa and to acknowledge all the hard work it had taken to get the authorities to relax the laws, allowing him to compete in the first place.

Papwa and I went on to become good friends and would often meet and play practice rounds. I wasn't the only one to take an interest: Gary arranged a number of invites to tournaments in the USA. Unfortunately, he became homesick and returned home after only competing once.

His game was best suited to the links courses and coastal conditions and, although certain reporters maintained that he was the third or fourth best player that has ever come out of South Africa, in my opinion, although he was very good, he more likely ranked in the top 25. I saw him on a number of occasions later on in life, but by that stage he had put on weight and was drinking heavily. Although I wasn't surprised to hear that he had died a few years later, I was sad. I always had the impression that he could have gone down as one of the best golfers in the world had he been blessed with the right opportunities from a much younger age.

Chapter Eleven

GAMBLING AND HORSE RACING

W E LEFT the Johannesburg area in 1971 and moved to Durban where we bought a home in La Lucia. I was appointed head coach at Windsor Park where I ran the Pro Shop and gave lessons. Obviously this impacted my finances – I was used to making a great deal of money in the US and earning less took some getting used to, although I did continue to participate in the Sunshine Circuit for the next four or five years and won a few smaller tournaments. I'm not suggesting that I was broke – I wasn't. I owned a home in one of Durban's more exclusive suburbs and my sons were all enrolled in Clifton, an excellent private school. However, I certainly wasn't living the high life any more and that was something that I had to learn to deal with.

I had become very involved in gambling and eventually partnered with a guy called Cyril Bradshaw and opened a bookmaking business. To be frank, we weren't great bookmakers, but the business paid for our gambling losses. I had always loved horses and became friendly with a number of top trainers including Herman Brown. I went on to coach his son Herman Junior who eventually played off a plus four handicap at the Kloof Country Club.

Gambling and horse racing, undoubtedly, gave me the same adrenalin rush as golf did. I used to spend a lot of time watching the horses train and got to know a winner when I saw one. A particular horse named Gate Crasher caught my eye. He was a magnificent animal (basically a replica of the great American horse Secretariat). Herman was convinced that he would win the Durban July, the most famous horse race on the South African racing calendar, that year and I realised that I could make a lot of money by backing him.

It so happened that Nikki had fallen in love with a property that was situated next door to the world renown Oppenheimer family's home in La Lucia. It was on the market for R88,000 (approximately $7,600) – a pittance compared to what it would be worth today considering that properties in this area now sell for tens of millions of rands. I knew that if I won R100,000 at the Durban July, I'd be able to buy the home for her; I didn't have the R7,000 needed for the bet, but thought I could pay it off at the bookmakers if the horse lost. I was elated when Gate Crasher crossed the line first, but came crashing down to earth when I heard there had been an objection. Gate Crasher had apparently carried Distinctly, the horse that had come third, to the outside, thus raising the objection. I knew that there was a good chance that the race was going to be taken away from Gate Crasher and that the horse that came second, Principal Boy which, ironically, was owned by the Oppenheimer family, would be crowned the winner. As things stood I got 4/1 at the bookmakers, if Principal Boy ended up winning and quickly took out another bet backing Principal Boy and, instead of losing, managed to win about R20,000. Nikki may not have got her house, but I was incredibly relieved to get my money back.

My three sons were excelling at sport at school. Bobby Jnr became fanatical about golf from about the age of eight or nine. Bradley was an exceptional swimmer and had mastered the butterfly stroke: he smashed Clifton's 30-year record by 10 seconds. The school's coach told us that he would undoubtedly become a Springbok if he continued his swimming. Darren on the other hand was a good cricketer. Like Bobby Jnr the two younger boys also loved golf and all three of them regularly played together after school.

Golf obviously still played an enormous role in my life and I finally earned my Springbok colours 19 years after I should have. In 1978, I was selected to play in the World Cup with Nicky Price in Hawaii. It was my second trip to Hawaii and what an amazing trip it was. We played on the island of Kauai, which was a long, long way away from home. After spending an unscheduled night in Honolulu, because of unruly demonstrators, we continued our journey. Anti-Apartheid demonstrations were in full swing at that stage, and the fact that South Africans were participating in the World Cup had really stirred things up.

We arrived in Princeville, Kauai the next morning and were met at the airport by a friend of Nikki's from Zimbabwe (then called Rhodesia). On the way to our hotel he stopped at the secluded beach where the movie *South Pacific* had been filmed, which just so happened to be my favourite musical of all time. The beach was stunningly beautiful. There wasn't a soul in sight and I couldn't resist stripping off all my clothes and diving into the crystal clear waters.

After my swim we booked in to our six-star condominium for a well-needed rest. The next day we arrived at the golf course refreshed and ready for action and discovered that we had two large, overweight, armed security guards assigned to us for protection. These two guys, who had probably never picked up a golf club in their lives, had to walk 18 holes dressed in suits and wearing leather-soled shoes. By the time we were finished they were sweating profusely and were absolutely exhausted. I felt genuinely sorry for the two of them and approached the tournament director and asked if he could provide them with a golf cart to use; he was nice enough to agree. The security guards got us back to the condo safe and sound and as a way of thanks promised to make us breakfast the next morning. True to their word, they arrived with bacon, eggs and juice and proceeded to make us a slap-up meal. They also brought us a couple of dozen beers for later in the day. We spent the day hitting balls and practising, while the guys enjoyed the shade of the golf cart watching us play. That evening we sat with them for an hour or two drinking beers and talking about things in general.

I had always been interested in guns and noticed that the one guy had a pretty neat .357 Magnum. He said he had a buddy in town who sold them, if I was interested in buying one. The next morning, he arrived with a collector's piece: an eight and three quarter inch nickel-plated Smith and Wesson Magnum in a walnut case with a hundred rounds of ammunition. The guns were very cheap and the Rand to Dollar exchange rate was about even at the time. This meant that I paid about R250 for the gun. Planning ahead, I thought I would put the gun in my golf bag and when I got to a South African airport I would declare the gun and ammunition. I would then get a licence, pay the duty and claim my gun back from the airport.

While in Kauai we had an unexpected early day after we finished playing golf and went to the beach. We had bought some flippers and goggles and wanted to do some spearfishing. The detectives stayed in their car while keeping an eye on us all the time. The store owner who sold us the gear warned us not to cross the coral reef as it was extremely deep with lots of sharks. I was snorkelling with my spear gun, chasing a brightly coloured fish, which through my goggles looked like a ten pounder. The fish kept avoiding me, darting in and out of the rocks with me in hot pursuit. The next thing I remember was looking down into a bottomless pit. In all the excitement of the chase, I hadn't realised that I'd crossed the reef and was now in dangerous waters. I started to swim towards the reef. I was a good, strong swimmer at the time but soon realised that the current was taking me further away. I went into overdrive and reached the coral in half a dozen frantic strokes. As I got onto the rocks a big black shape dived into the water right next to me. It was Nicky Price who wanted to scare the living daylights out of me. He succeeded – my heart nearly stopped with fright. He thought it was hilarious and was still laughing about the incident hours later.

We didn't play particularly well in the World Cup and ended in either sixth or seventh place. I'm not for one moment suggesting that the ongoing demonstrations caused us to lose; however, trying to play a game of golf under these circumstances was not a pleasant experience at all. People would call us names and shout profanities as we made our way around the course, and things heated up even more when we walked off the 18th at the end of the day.

Despite all of the drama, it was an unbelievable experience overall that was managed extremely well by a group of wonderful people. I was so taken with the place that I asked the golf pro at the club whether he had a job for me, explaining that this was where I wanted to spend the rest of my life – sadly it was not to be and all too soon it was time for me to wend my way back to South Africa. Before I left I bought a new golf bag and a new set of irons. I donated my old ones to under-privileged kids who couldn't afford to play golf.

We prepared ourselves for a very long flight back to South Africa: flying from Kauai to Honolulu, on to San Francisco, to New York, then to Madrid. Believe it or not, this worked out to be the quickest and easiest way to get back to Johannesburg. From Johannesburg we had to take a connecting flight to Cape Town where we were to tee off in the South African Open at Mowbray Golf Club that same day.

On the flight from New York to Madrid, we met up with an American fighter pilot who was stationed in Madrid. We told him about our seven-hour stop-over. He mentioned that he had an apartment across from the airport where we could rest, have a shower and a sleep before our flight home. This was a very kind, very welcome gesture. As we got in to Madrid, we realised that although Nicky had a British passport and would be able to enter Spain, I was travelling on a South African passport and unfortunately did not have a visa to enter the country. We had been travelling for 30 hours and were exhausted. However, although I begged and pleaded with the guys at passport control to let me take advantage of the hot shower and bed on offer, the authorities wouldn't budge and refused to allow me entry. Nicky, great friend that he is, never left my side and decided not to go on his own, we spent the time waiting for the next flight on a couple of uncomfortable airport seats.

On the flight to Johannesburg, we were told that the plane had to make an emergency stopover in Zaire, Tanzania, to pick up a number of injured workers who had been involved in a factory fire. They needed to be transported to South Africa for treatment and the crew made a make-shift emergency tent at the back of the plane, making the injured as comfortable as possible.

The sporting authorities were made aware of the delay and made arrangements to ensure that we made our connecting flight to Cape Town in time. We arrived in Cape Town 47 hours after we left Hawaii, utterly exhausted, but just in time to take a shower and get into clean clothes. We loosened up by hitting a few balls and were ready to start our game. As I walked off the second tee after my drive, the caddy, a Cape Coloured called 'Whitey', called to me that my bag was very heavy saying *'Nei, Master, die sak is swaar, man!'* ('No, boss, this bag is heavy, man'). I told him that he was getting old and that he should just shut up and carry the bag.

And suddenly the reality hit me. I unzipped the bag and saw the bullets and gun case in the side pocket. I realised, with a shock, that with all the ushering through customs in Johannesburg, I had completely forgotten about the gun. I told Whitey that it was a souvenir and that I would pay him extra if he carried the bag all the way to the end.

Nicky and I possibly played two of the best rounds of golf ever, each scoring 71, which, considering that we hadn't seen a bed for two days and had crossed numerous time zones, wasn't too shabby. We flew back to Johannesburg the following week, where I took the gun and bullets and hid them in the ceiling of my house. A couple of months later, I heard that the government had launched an amnesty programme for unlicensed firearms – in other words no questions as to how the gun was acquired would be asked. I took the .357 to Randburg police station and walked into the office of the Commander, who to my surprise knew my name. It turned he was also a keen golfer and he immediately wanted to know the story behind the gun. He laughed like a drain, issued the license and a few months later I sold the R250 gun for about R4,000.

Jock Verwey and Bobby Locke

Jock Verwey and Gary Player

A

Bobby Verwey

Bobby and Nicolette

B

Bobby and Nicolette's wedding

Bobby, Nikki, Pat and Harold Henning

C

*Retief Waltman, Gary Player, Arnold Palmer, Bobby
Verwey: Royal Birkdale Golf Club, UK, 1961*

Jack Burke Jnr, Bobby, Gary Player, Jack Nicklaus

Jock Verwey, Darren Verwey, Bobby Verwey Snr, Bradley Verwey and Bobby Verwey Jnr

Bobby Verwey Jnr, Bobby Verwey Snr

E

Bob Charles, Bobby Verwey Jnr, Gary Player

F

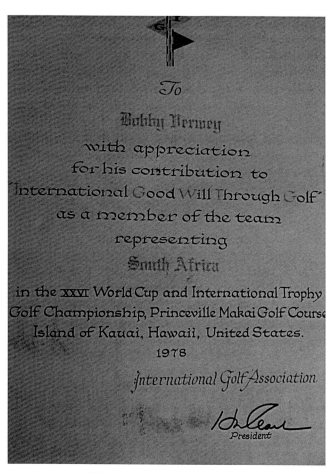

To

Bobby Verwey

with appreciation
for his contribution to
International Good Will Through Golf
as a member of the team
representing

South Africa

in the XXVI World Cup and International Trophy
Golf Championship, Princeville Makai Golf Course
Island of Kauai, Hawaii, United States.
1978

International Golf Association

President

World Cup Merit Certificate

G

Lawrence Batley handing cup to Bobby, Huddersfield, UK

Bobby and Jack Nicklaus

H

Karsten Solheim, owner of PING, with Bobby

Bobby and Bob Troskey

I

Kevin Costner with Bobby

Robert Wagner and Bobby

J

Chapter Twelve

RUBBING SHOULDERS WITH THE RICH AND FAMOUS

GARY AND Vivienne took my mom overseas with them on many occasions, so she could spend time with the children, while Vivienne watched Gary play. At one particular Pro-Am tournament dinner, my mom met the actor Robert Wagner. He was so nice and even dished up and brought her food to her. She was so impressed by him and gave him a peck on the cheek to thank him.

A few years later I was playing in the Monte Carlo Open on top of the mountain: a very impressive golf course with amazing views over Monaco. The first time I was there, I walked into the bar near the yacht basin and there he was sitting with his wife, Jill St John. I walked up to him, and gave him a kiss on the cheek. He looked at me in amusement when I told him that was from my mother, Gary Player's mother-in-law. I mentioned that she had never forgotten how he had spoiled her a few years earlier. He recalled what a lovely lady she was and later we took a picture of the two of us which he signed: 'To granny, from Robert Wagner'.

It was an unforgettable week as I also met Kevin Costner, had a few drinks with him and got to know him well in the week we were there. Another absolutely wonderful man and a gentleman.

One evening after golf we got a ride to take us down the mountain. I bumped into another actor, Jason Bateman, who it so happened I had given a golf lesson to several years earlier in Charlotte, North Carolina. When I walked up to him and said hello, he looked at me and said that he could not remember my name, but he could never forget my voice.

I then drove down with him and his girlfriend in a courtesy car to the hotel. A large number of famous people were playing in the tournament including the likes of Prince Albert of Monaco, Sir Richard Branson, the founder of the Virgin group of companies, the James Bond actor Sir Roger Moore and Patrick Duffy of *Dallas* fame, to name a few.

The following day we walked into the clubhouse where all the VIPs were sitting. I saw a very well-known face at the bottom of the table and asked someone who it was. They told me it was J. P. MacManus. I exclaimed: 'Oh my word!'

Some 15 years before this event, I was at the Sandown racetrack in London, busy losing my shirt – I was about £2,000 down and was desperately looking to back a winner in order to recoup some of my losses. I needed a good tip from an owner, a trainer or anyone else who was in the know. The friend I was with pointed to a guy dressed in a raincoat who was standing a short distance away and told me I should ask him. I walked up to him introduced myself, told him I was losing a lot of money and asked if he could please tell me if the horse I wanted to back in the last race could win. He asked how much I was losing, so I told him. He said, 'Back the horse, bet enough to win £3,000 – it's sure to win.' I proceeded to back the horse, which went on to win the race by about ten or twelve lengths. As I looked around to thank him, he was nowhere to be seen.

It turned out that the shy guy sitting at the end of the table was the same man: J. P. MacManus. He was an extremely wealthy Irishman, known at the time as the biggest gambler in Europe. I walked over to him and as I got near, he stood up, held out his hand and said, 'Bobby Verwey, Sandown Racetrack, 1985. I told you to back the horse for £3,000.' I was absolutely floored, by his amazing memory. My only comeback to his was, 'J. P., do you have another winner for me?'

After such a fantastic week, I should have won the tournament, but sadly missed out.

Chapter Thirteen

AN UNFORTUNATE INCIDENT

B Y 1979, my marriage to Nikki had become very fragile and we started to lead separate lives. If truth be told, we had married far too young and outgrew one another. We sold the house in La Lucia and moved to Johannesburg where I built a very successful golf range. At around the same time my parents had become friends with a very wealthy businessman, Dave Morton, and his wife. They all loved to gamble and it wasn't long before Nikki and I became part of their circle and even came down to their holiday cottage in Southbroom on the South Coast of KwaZulu-Natal. Dave used to give Nikki large sums of money to gamble. Unbeknownst to me, he had fallen head over hills in love with her.

Our marriage troubles were deepening and we decided to permanently part ways. Dave Morton quickly divorced his third wife and he and Nikki married shortly after our divorce was finalised. She moved into his large house in Randburg and the boys went to live in the cottage on the property.

For the next few years, I used to pick them up every morning for school and drop them off again after school. Although I never liked Dave much, I have to acknowledge that he treated my boys well. He died of ALS in 2014. Nikki has always been a wonderful mother and I could never fault her for the love she has for our three sons.

I hated living on my own and it wasn't long before I became involved with a married woman, who was trapped in an unhappy marriage. The affair continued for about five or six years and at that point in time she was the best thing that could have happened to me. She wanted to divorce her husband and marry me, but I did not want to be the cause of her two young children being without their father. Our relationship ended and I moved on. I still believe it was the right thing to do, even though I adored her and believed she was my soulmate.

At around this time, Gary gave my father the rights to build a putt putt course on a vacant piece of land at Sun City. I think it was because Gary appreciated and was very grateful for everything that my father had done for him over the years. Everything was done in good faith with a verbal rather than a written contract in place. As I've said before, my father was an extremely talented man, who not only built the impressive course by hand, but also ploughed a great deal of money into the venture. He ran it quite successfully over the next few years.

The first ever Sun City Golf Classic was held in 1979, played on a golf course designed by Gary Player.

I finished runner-up in the tournament, one stroke behind my famous brother-in-law.

I was quoted after the tournament by some reporters where I criticised the kikuyu grass that was used on the fairways. Gary Player told the media that it was only my personal opinion and he didn't care what 'Bobby Verwey or any other pro thought and that they didn't have to play in the tournament again, if they felt so strongly about the grass.' Still, I wasn't the only one complaining. Sol Kerzner, who had developed Sun City, was upset when Graham Henning quipped that he would prefer to fight in the South African border war (this was still ongoing at the time) than go back onto that particular golf course again. At the time, Sol said that nobody could expect five-star conditions on a course, that had, until the year before, been a wilderness area.

The next golf course at the Lost City, which forms part of the massive Sun City hotel complex, was, however, a different story. While I'm not suggesting that Sol took my opinion on the grass to heart, this course featured a finer type of grass on its fairways.

To be fair, I have to say that I was totally wrong in my critique – kikuyu is most probably the only suitable drought resistant grass to use in these harsh, dry African Highveld conditions. The only reason that I found it difficult to play on this type of surface was because I am a short hitter. When you play on coarse kikuyu grass, the ball stays put without running on. In essence, I became an even shorter hitter playing under these conditions, which of course did my game no favours.

The World Cup is a major tournament and was originally founded by a Canadian industrialist, in the hope that it would promote international goodwill. The tournament started out as the Canada Cup in 1953, but the name was changed to the World Cup in 1967 and went on to become one of the most prestigious events on the golfing calendar. As things stand, around 14 different countries have brought home the trophy and many famous golfers like Jack Nicklaus, who won it six times, and Arnold Palmer, who won it five times, have fought hard for this sought-after trophy. The tournament has never been about the money – the prestige of taking part in the competition was far more important than any monetary gain. That said, the tournament was sponsored by the PGA and all our travel and accommodation costs were covered.

The 1980 World Cup tournament was played at El Ricon in Bogota, Colombia. Tienie Britz and I flew from Johannesburg to Miami, where we took a connecting flight to Bogota. We had a five- or six-hour stopover in Miami and I decided that it was the perfect place to show Tienie what the world of golf really looked like. We checked our baggage in at the airport and caught a cab to the Durrell Hotel and Country Club where we ate a fabulous lunch before descending on what has to be one of the finest pro shops I've ever visited. Needless to say that I ended up spending around $1,500 on new golf attire.

The city of Bogota was a city of extremes, housing both the very poor and the very rich. Crime levels were very high and as such the luxurious houses had towering 20 feet walls surrounding their properties.

Karsten Solheim, the founder of the PING golf club company, sat next to me every day during the hour-long trip to the golf course. I found him very interesting, but the other golfers mostly found him boring, as he was always talking about golf balls and shafts, clubs and the manufacturing side of woods, irons and putters. He was eccentric, but loved his job and I can understand why he became such a huge success. To this day manufacturers of golfing equipment duplicate his ideas, but back then his ideas were criticised and misunderstood. Like my father, he always maintained that the putter should have a seven-degree loft. It makes me laugh when I see players today, using one or two degree putters and then cannot comprehend why their balls bounce, complaining about imperfections on the greens.

Tienie and I played well and ended fourth. In those days only the first three places received prize money. First prize was $500, 2nd $250 and 3rd $100, which is pretty laughable when you consider what sponsors pay these days.

While flying back to South Africa, there was an incident in Bogota: the aircraft that was behind us as we left was hijacked to Cuba. As we came in to land at New York there was some security problem and we had to stay in the air, circling for more than an hour before landing. As a result, we missed our connecting flight to Johannesburg. Tienie and I went to collect our luggage, but mine was nowhere to be found. I only had the clothes I was wearing, but Tienie knew the Consul at the South African Consulate and he kindly put us up in his apartment. We ended up stranded in New York for three days. I called the airport every hour, but my suitcase with my brand new clothes never turned up. A year later, while I was playing golf in South Africa, I met the CEO of Pan American Airlines in Johannesburg, who told me that the tag must have come off in transit and in such instances would be stored at there lost baggage area. He phoned me a few days later to tell me that the suitcase had indeed been kept there, but had, because the policy of only storing lost baggage for a year, been sold on auction two days prior to his enquiry. Someone must have bought all my brand new, never worn clothes for next to nothing and got himself a real bonus.

Chapter Fourteen

A FRIEND IN NEED

I PLAYED in the Irish Open at Royal Dublin in 1980. Just before the final round in Dublin one of the sponsors came to me and asked if I wanted to play in the Pro-Am at Galway Bay the next day. I was travelling with Nicky Price, so asked him if there was room for Nicky to play as well. He said they would love it if he also took part. He drove us to Galway Bay.

On the way, we stopped off at a world-renowned salmon restaurant and he was not wrong about the food there being incredible. As we continued on our way in the pitch dark, we came over the crest of a rise, and in front of me was a sight I will never forget: the whole of Galway Bay was in front of us and the full moon was casting a bright silvery reflection on the water. It reminded me of my late father, whose favourite song was 'Galway Bay'. I asked the driver if he could sing this song for us. It was a stupid question, as there is probably not an Irishman alive who doesn't know this song. He was the singer in his brother's band and he immediately obliged by singing in the most unbelievable voice. With the moon over Galway Bay and the haunting song sung by my fellow traveller, I had tears running down my face as I thought of my father. He would have loved hearing this song in this magical place.

The next morning, we were up at daybreak to play in the tournament. We were playing very early as there was an airline strike in Ireland and we had to be driven back to Dublin to catch a flight to London for a connecting flight to Switzerland. As I walked into the clubhouse I saw the display of prizes on a table. In the middle was the biggest Waterford crystal vase that I had ever seen, about two-thirds of a metre in height and absolutely magnificent. I asked one of the organisers what that prize was for, he said it would be for the best pro on the day. I asked what would happen if there was a tie? He said each pro would then get one. I played brilliant golf on that very cold and windy day and three-putted the eighteenth green to score 67, which I thought would get me that vase. We left immediately after the last hole as we had to go to Dublin and I was to phone from Dublin to find out who had won. About an hour into our journey we heard on the radio that a bomb had tragically killed Lord Mountbatten. By the time we eventually got into London, I phoned the organisers and was told that the last guy shot 66 and beat me by one. I still cry over that beautifully crafted Waterford crystal vase.

I was playing in the Big Falls Classic in Zimbabwe and in the evenings a couple of friends and I were busy gambling at the casino. At the end of the week my friends and I owed the casino 7,000 Zimbabwean dollars. They said I could pay the money on the Monday in Harare at the Meikles Hotel. Mark McNulty who was also playing in the Classic came over to me and gave me Z$7,000 in cash to pay the debt and asked if I could repay him in South Africa with SA currency instead. On the Tuesday morning, I took the money he gave me and paid the casino.

I then went to the local Tattersall club to bet on horse racing that was taking place in South Africa. I was friendly with a number of bookmakers there, had quite a good day and ended up winning about Z$1,000. After dinner that evening, I was having a beer in my room, when there was a knock on my door. It was the currency police, wanting to know where I got the Z$7,000 to pay for the debt at the Meikles Hotel. If I told them that I got the money from Mark McNulty, they would have locked him up for a very long time as this was regarded as being a very serious offense. Thinking on my feet, I told them that I went to the horse racing the day before and won the money on the horses. I was in a state of panic and knew that they were surely going to try and find out if this was true. I phoned a really good bookmaker friend of mine, asking him to find out who had a good strike on one or two horses the previous day. He phoned the next morning to tell me about a couple of bookmakers who had a few good bets and that they would tell the currency police that I had placed the bet. That evening, the police came for another visit and said they had checked on my story at the bookmakers and it was conceivable that I had won the money. They would give me the benefit of the doubt, but mentioned that they did think I was pulling the wool over their eyes and to never try that again.

Mark McNulty and I had never been very good friends, but I am sure he would, after reading this, realise what a close shave he had.

It would be wrong of me not to mention my two good friends from Zimbabwe, Aidan and Val Knight, who lived in Bulawayo and always made me feel part of the family when I was there. Aidan's two sons fought in the bush war in Zimbabwe. Later, when Robert Mugabe took the farms away from the majority of white farmers, Aidan and Val came to live in Johannesburg, where we reignited our friendship. Aiden died a number of years ago, but was a really good friend and a real character of note. Val, I believe, is living in Cape Town now, with her gorgeous daughter, Veronica. She laughingly told me years later how she always had a crush on me from the age of twelve.

One year, after finishing another golf tournament in Zimbabwe, Aidan took Bobby Cole and myself hunting. Bobby Cole was a phenomenal shot and as we were walking along, a kudu (a kind of antelope) broke out of the bush on the right and Bobby, who was a left-handed shot, let rip towards the kudu. He thought he had hit the animal but didn't bring it down. We had trackers and when they got to the spot where the kudu was, they found blood stains. We tracked for a short while, but could not stay too long, as we had a plane to catch back to South Africa. Aidan phoned me that night to tell me that they found the dead kudu and that it was a fatal shot. This was the last hunt I ever went on – today I am fanatical about wildlife conservation and spend a lot of time in South Africa's many beautiful game reserves.

Bobby Cole and I were great friends for many years and today he is the teaching pro at Doral Country Club in Miami, Florida. We had always been very good friends with Lee Trevino – and apart from being a great golfer, Lee was, in my book, the greatest entertainer in the golfing world. People loved him as he joked and laughed his way around the golf course.

One of the stories he told was that he was so ugly as a child that his mom tied a bone around his neck so that the dog would play with him. Another was that once, when he was getting onto a bus, the driver told him, 'Blacks at the back of the bus.'

Lee told him, 'I'm not black, I'm Mexican!'

The driver replied, 'In that case, get off the bus!'

However, one of the most famous stories of all was when he teed up in the last round of the British Open with Tony Jacklin. Lee, who was known to be very talkative when he played, was told by Tony that it was a very important tournament for him and said, 'Lee, hope you don't mind if I don't speak.'

Lee then told him: 'Tony, you don't have to say a word, just listen… '

Lee went on to win the tournament after a lot of drama on the 17th hole. Lee was over the green in four shots and Tony was fifteen feet away from the pin in three. Lee proceeded to chip the ball into the hole for a par five and Tony putted a par three. However, Lee went on to win by one.

In fact, Lee wrote a book where he mentioned my achievements on the longest golf course on the tour, Hazeltine in Minneapolis, Minnesota, where I had a fantastic tournament. I lost by one shot to Lew Graham. I held the course record there for a number of years. It was so funny as I was a short hitter and this was a particularly difficult and long course and did not suit my game at all.

He came to South Africa quite a few times to play exhibition matches with Gary Player and also played in a few local tournaments. He won the Sun City Classic and also competed in the Million Dollar Tournament without ever winning it. In 1980, at the age of 14 years, my son Bobby Verwey Jnr was a scratch handicap golfer. Lee met Bobby Jnr, who was always with me, and they also became firm friends. When Lee visited South Africa, each time he left, he would give my golf-mad son his golf bag, caps, balls and gloves. One year, Lee was invited to play in the Nedbank Million Dollar Tournament at Sun City as one of eight or ten players that same year. I thought that if Lee wasn't bringing his own caddy, Bobby Jnr could get the chance to caddy for him. A couple of weeks before the tournament, I phoned to ask him; he agreed and loved the idea. Bobby Jnr and I went to Sun City for a couple of days to look at the greens, rolled balls around to determine the swings as well as taking a lot of measurements on the fairways. The tournament was paying the winner $1,000,000 and about $100,000 for the loser. Of course the caddies shared in any big win and would receive a good cut. This could have been a lot of money for Bobby, which would then kick-start his golfing career and take him overseas to play in bigger tournaments. I wasn't a wealthy man and saw this as a great opportunity for my son.

However, when I told Gary, who was in charge of the tournament, Gary refused, saying that he only wanted black caddies to caddy because this would be seen as good exposure for South Africa. He had his own black caddy and I, albeit reluctantly, initially saw his point. However, after our chat he suddenly saw an opportunity to promote his own two sons. One son, Wayne, who was a very good golfer, ended up caddying for Johnny Miller, who went on to win the tournament and his other son, who didn't actually play golf, caddied for Jack Nicklaus. Unfortunately, it appears that nepotism and the lure of big money played a huge role in not giving my son his big chance on that day.

Gary, Mark McNulty and the man who had founded Sun City, Sol Kerzner, were on hand to meet Lee when he arrived at the hotel. Unfortunately, so was my father Jock and he proceeded to give them all a piece of his mind and made it quite clear to all and sundry that he thought Gary's decision was grossly unfair.

At about this time Mark was just about to take over his father's empire, Black Knight Industries. We will never know whether my father's outburst on that day caused him to fall out of favour with the Players. But, a year or two year later, my father received a notification to say that his lease on the putt putt course had run out and he had to give it back to the Player family. They paid him out – but in my opinion the paltry sum they offered didn't come anywhere near the blood, sweat and tears my father had poured into the venture. My father was unhappy about the whole thing, but without a contract there was little he could do.

Chapter Fifteen

ACCUSED AND SUSPENDED

THE FOLLOWING year, I again played in the Sun City Golf Classic. The day before the start of the Classic, forty of the pros were chosen to play with the sponsors and their clients in a Pro-Am tournament. I was partnered with business tycoon, Dr Johan Rupert, one of the richest men in Africa, the chairman of Remgro among other companies and a couple of his ultra-rich friends. He introduced me to his lovely fiancée, Gaynor, who today is his wife – a stunningly beautiful lady.

Dr Rupert sponsored the Dunhill Invitational Tournaments in Scotland and the Dunhill Open at Leopard Creek. He is a very generous man, particularly to the golfing fraternity in South Africa, helping the younger players to participate in some tournaments. I was honoured to be his partner on this occasion.

Dr Rupert told me that he had a couple of big bets with some of the other teams and if we won, I was in for a huge payday. As it turned out, it was quite a large incentive to me, as I shot 64 that day and we won the Pro-Am. However, 33 years later, I am still waiting for that payday he promised me. They say the rich become richer and the poor become poorer. I can see now how that happens.

The next year I was still on a high, playing very good golf in the Classic. Coming into the last round I was again well-placed, only a couple of shots behind the leader. I turned up at the golf course, but it was raining cats and dogs and play was held up for about two or three hours. I was playing with Tertius Claassen from South Africa and Glen Ralph, an English pro.

When I got to the 15th hole I was six under par for the round and really challenging for the lead. I hit my second shot about four metres to the right of the pin, where there was a wet patch between me and the hole. Here the top dressing was washed out and formed a huge indentation on the green.

I should have waited for the other players to join me on the green, but being impatient, I didn't, as it would have taken at least an hour or more for the ruling... so I moved the ball. I two-putted for a par and as I walked off the green, Glen Ralph came up to me and said that his girlfriend saw me move the ball half an inch nearer to the hole. This was a blatant lie, as I actually moved it two metres to the left, at exactly the same distance from the hole. This was only done in order to move it away from the muddy ground. With hindsight I realised that it was a very stupid thing to do, as I could have putted two balls out. It would have been the best thing to do and would have been the end of the story. I parred the last three holes and shot 66 which would have placed me in third spot.

After I finished, I told Jimmy Hemphill, who was the tournament director, that I was accused of moving the ball. I had also been on the course for eight hours and said that I was cold, wet and hungry and desperately wanted to have a bath. He told me it was fine and not to worry; they would call me to discuss it as soon as the last players finished for the day. I went to my room, took a hot bath, had something to eat and dressed in dry clothes.

About an hour later, I still had not heard from the PGA and returned to the 18th green to see what was happening. I then saw on the board that I had been disqualified, without any hearing or without anyone listening to my side of the story. When I went to confront Jimmy, he told me he had called my room and that there was no reply. I asked him what number he had called and as it turned out it was my parent's room number, but they were in the casino and not in their room.

I employed a lawyer straight after the tournament and was given a hearing the following week in Cape Town, as this was where our next tournament was to be played. I had my lawyer with me, but they had to have a full committee and as they did not have one there, I was not allowed to play that week. They organised another meeting for me in Johannesburg where I was going to be given a fair hearing by the tournament committee. I went to the meeting with my lawyer and advocate; the PGA also had their lawyer present. Then I stood up to state my case and told them my story, as well as the way I usually play and how I would penalise myself, when I thought it was necessary. Their lawyer said that I had such a strong case that there was no way that I could lose the appeal. When I went back into the room, they found me guilty and suspended me for two years. I found a top trial lawyer, Fanie Cilliers, and sued the PGA for wrongful verdict. We took them to court, where I won the case by a proverbial mile, plus expenses. The Judge ruled that as I did not have a fair hearing, they were liable for all costs.

The PGA said they would give me another hearing. Then I heard that it would be the exact same committee who found me guilty in the first case and I would have to pay for Glen Ralph and his girlfriend to return from overseas to give evidence. I would have to go to Sun City, pay all accommodation and air fares – at the time about R100,000. Win or lose, I would have to cover all my own expenses. I did not for one minute think that the same committee would come to a different conclusion, therefore, as I did not have that kind of money to defend my honour yet again, conceded defeat.

I've always felt that Gary could have used his influence, but sadly he was not seen or heard from in this difficult time and never came to my aid when I so desperately needed it. All he had to do was put in a good word for me or maybe ask them to rather fine me instead of the two-year suspension. He was a god in the golfing world and as such it would have been possible for him to change this extremely harsh verdict. These thoughts kept going through my mind as it was a humiliating slap in the face and this from the man who used to be like a brother to me – I mean we were after all family...

While I wish I could say that bridges have been mended, sadly I'm not as close to Gary or my sister as I'd like to be – some may think that this is due to envy. It's not! I have always and will always admire the man. I may not have always agreed with the way he conducted himself on and off the greens, but he has been a good husband to Vivienne and a terrific father to my nieces and nephews and of course, he is still an exceptional golfer. I'm not totally sure when things started to turn sour between the two of us, but fortunately this has not affected the relationship he has with my sons, particularly Bobby Jnr, who has gone on to caddy for him on a number of occasions.

Regardless of what was happening on the family front, I was determined not to allow the suspension to get me down. I've always had a positive mind and I dug deep and came back stronger than ever before – particularly on the Senior Tour eight years later.

Chapter Sixteen

THE BRITISH SENIOR OPEN

FOUR OR five years after my divorce, while still in a relationship with the married lady I mentioned earlier, I met Isobel Jeans, a great show-jumper and a horse-riding teacher. It so happened that a friend of mine, James Goodman, a racehorse trainer, and his wife Susan told her about me, mentioning that I could teach her how to play golf. She started coming to me for golf lessons, took one look at me and started chasing me big time. At that time, I broke off my extra-marital affair and started dating Isobel.

With hindsight, and knowing what is common knowledge today – I'm still flummoxed as to why she ever made a play for me.

After I had coached her for about a year, she eventually turned out to be a very good golfer. She had always dreamt of owning her own stables and riding school and I was instrumental in her buying a ten-hectare property in Diepsloot, near Johannesburg: arranging the mortgage, paying the deposit and also paying the monthly instalments.

I wasn't in love initially, but I eventually did grow to love her. She had been married before but did not have any children of her own. We got married in 1987 and lived on the property, where she gave horse-riding lessons and practised her show jumping. In my opinion, it was just about the most perfect place to live. I'd been involved with horses all my life and had developed a love for horses from an early age. I also started riding from time to time. I can honestly say that Isobel became my best friend – unfortunately she didn't get along with any of my sons and, although I'm not sure whether they picked up on this, they never liked her either.

I bought more horses for her and started improving the property with a swimming pool, new kitchen and bathrooms as well as adding more stables. I spent a fortune on a secure fence around the property and settled down to a life with my new wife. She was kept busy with horse-riding lessons and I still played all the major tournaments in South Africa and some abroad. I took her overseas with me more than twenty times as well as taking her mother to her home country of Portugal on two separate occasions. The trips weren't always golf related and although she caddied for me on a couple of occasions when I started playing overseas in the Senior Tour, I did send her overseas to visit friends. A few years after we were married, I bought the ten-hectare property next door to Isobel's and transformed it into the Verwey Driving Range. My son Bradley started working for me at the driving range while Darren, who was still at school, stayed with his mother.

Bobby Jnr was, at this stage, really beginning to shine as a golfer and at the age of seventeen played in an under-21 amateur tournament at ERPM. He won by fourteen shots, with Ernie Els coming a distant second. He went on to play in Europe as an amateur before turning pro at the age of 18 and playing and winning a number of Winter Tour events along with the Club Pro Championship. By the time he was 21 he was running the second Bobby Verwey Driving Range that we had built in Waterkloof, Pretoria.

My first senior tour, at the age of fifty years and five months, was at Royal Lytham and St Anne's Golf Club in 1991. This was the course where I first played as an amateur in 1958. I had fallen in love with the golf course all those years ago and told anyone who would listen that no one was going to beat me there again. I was putting very poorly before the tour, but thankfully Jamie Gouffe, who just so happened to be working as a golf instructor at my driving range, came to the rescue by giving me a seriously good putting lesson. That lesson was the reason how and why I won the Senior Open. Today he is a top coach for American and European Tour players and follows them around the world.

I will be forever grateful for the most important lesson he gave me. He basically told me to look at the hole when putting, and that was the answer to my putting poorly. I putted like this for the rest of the tournament with huge success.

Ten days before the Senior Open, I played at Cranes-Montana in Switzerland in the annual Olivier

Barras tournament. It was the site of the Swiss Open and is where the European Open (at which I had a number of previous good finishes and once held the course record of 62) is played. I finished the Barras Tournament in the top ten, which was a mini-European event.

This gave me enormous confidence, which followed me to the British Senior Open. I played really well from the first day. In the third round I teed off with Gary and Bob Charles and gave both of them a good lesson in golf. In the final round I was drawn to play with Tommy Horton and Peter Butler. They were both Ryder Cup players and Tommy in particular desperately wanted to win the British Senior Open. At the start of the round, I was quite keyed up but reasonably calm and surprisingly confident. I didn't play as well as I had in the previous three rounds, but some great short game work kept me in the lead. I remember on the sixteenth hole hitting my second shot over the green, but then chipped back about three metres (ten feet) short of the hole. While I was surveying the putt, I was totally in the zone. I had no fear that I would miss the putt. Tommy was two shots behind me. I hit the putt right in the middle of the hole. Leading by two shots, I then had a good drive from the seventeenth. When you play your second shot from here, the pin is not visible. It is amazing how certain thoughts enter your mind. My mind went back to Gary, who years earlier, had nearly lost the British Open when he hooked his shot into thick rough. The time to take the shot had nearly expired when his caddy Rabbit, who was an ex-professional basketball player, found the ball in the grass. The entire episode was rather controversial as there was speculation that Rabbit had dropped the ball. Be that as it may, Gary won the tournament, which just goes to show that by having nerves of steel and truly believing in yourself, you can get to the winning line.

Guarding against going left, I hit a three iron on my second shot to the right of the green into a bunker, and dropped a shot to par, which was a five. When I got to the 72nd hole I was leading by one stroke. Tommy drove off first and hit a snap hook off the tee, and got lucky when it bounced over two or three deep bunkers, finishing about a hundred yards left of the fairway, in a position where he could still get his second shot onto the green. I thought that I had hit a very good drive, but it was very close to the bunker (the same bunker where Brown and Luiz were both trying to hit from in 1958). I walked into the bunker with a sand iron and played a bunker shot, back onto the fairway. When I got to my ball, I had 137 yards to the pin. While I was waiting to play my third shot, Tommy hit his second shot onto the front edge of the green at least 135 feet from the hole.

When I played my third shot, I was very incredibly cool, calm and collected. I hit the most gorgeous nine iron, straight at the pin. In the midst of screams of delight and people milling around, I could not see what happened to the ball. Walking towards the green, hoping beyond all hope that my ball had landed about six inches from the pin. It wasn't to be and as I walked onto the green I was very disappointed to find my ball had landed at least two metres away from the hole. Tommy Horton putted about a metre short of the hole and when I looked up at the scoreboard I realised I needed to sink this putt to beat Tommy Horton and Bob Charles by one stroke.

It was a great feeling walking up just knowing in my heart that I was not going to miss this putt. Before I putted, I looked up over the crowd and saw Bob Charles on the steps of the scoring trailer, anxiously watching me. I looked directly at him and made a thumbs down sign at him. It was a bit arrogant, but perhaps understandable, given that on several occasions I had to be satisfied with second place when he beat me.

When I eventually got to the putt and lined it up, I felt incredibly calm. For a millisecond the thought occurred to me that the crowd was eerily quiet and that this must indicate how immensely important this putt must be. As the ball landed in the hole, the crowd roared as I fell on my back, dressed in my pink trousers and a white sweater on to the green. As I stood up to look triumphantly at Bob Charles, he had gone. Tommy Horton later became the best senior player, for many a year, but sadly he never felt the incredible pleasure of winning the Senior Open. I was elated by the win, particularly because at the age of 50 years and five months I was the youngest player ever to do so, but have to say that the importance of winning such a major tournament only really dawned on me later.

At the prize giving afterwards, I suggested to the Royal and Ancient Golf Club (R&A) officials that they should give the winner of the Senior Open an invite to the British Open a week later. To my mind, seeing how the older players could compete with younger up and coming players would make for an exciting game of golf. I knew there were many senior golfers around the world who would love to see this happening and that something like this would surely boost the game – the R&A thought it was a great idea. Sadly, I got the short end of the stick and this only happened from the year following my win. Interestingly, the United States Golf Association (USGA) promptly followed suit and these days anyone who wins the US seniors automatically receives an invite to the US Open.

Chapter Seventeen

BETRAYED

AFTERWARDS AT the prize-giving my sister, Vivienne, invited me to have dinner with her at the hotel. Gary, Arnold Palmer and Bob Charles had already flown to an exhibition match and so I joined the ladies for a celebratory dinner.

It was quite an experience walking into the dining area, neatly dressed in collar and tie, with Isobel and seeing everyone there giving me a standing ovation. My first prize for winning the British Senior Open was my biggest win ever, about £25,000... and also my proudest achievement.

The next day, I took Isobel to a tack shop where I bought her £2,500 worth of jodhpurs, bridles, riding equipment and bits, as payment for her having caddied for me. I subsequently heard from a friend of Arnold Palmer that he had a £50 bet on me to sink the putt. Coming from the king of golf, it was another great compliment by one of my well-admired peers.

A number of years later I had an invitation to play in the Charlie Pride Invitational in Albuquerque, New Mexico.

Charlie was a very well-known country and western singer. The day before the tournament, I was sitting in the coffee shop when he walked in. I got up to thank him for the invitation and to introduce myself. He started laughing and said: 'Bobby Verwey, how can I ever forget that name, when I saw you with pink trousers and white sweater falling on your back after winning the British Senior Open.'

Regretfully, at that point in time, there were only two senior tournaments, the British Senior Open and the British Senior PGA. I went to the British Open at Turnberry as a spectator and also because my sponsors wanted me to make an appearance there after winning the British Senior Open. When I walked onto the practice tee to watch some of my friends hitting balls, they all came up to congratulate me on winning the tournament. Nicky Price, Fulton Allen, Ernie Els, Hugh Baiocchi, Retief Goosen all shook my hand, but Greg Norman just turned his back on all of us and kept hitting golf balls.

It didn't come as surprise that he didn't join the others in congratulating me; in Australia he was known as the most unpopular golf pro amongst most players. His nerve was also questionable – for example one year he was leading in all four of the major tournaments going in to the final round, but never won any one of them. His private life, in my opinion, also left a lot to be desired.

After the Senior Open, Gary did arrange some invites for me to a few tournaments. The first one was in New York City where I received VIP treatment on the back of winning the Senior Open. I remember walking onto the practice tee where I saw a young paraplegic boy called Albert sitting in his wheelchair. When he saw me, he shouted, 'Congratulations, Mr Bobby, for winning the British Senior Open.' That was a very special compliment to be recognised by someone like that. I took his wheelchair from his mother, and wheeled him onto the practice tee. At least a dozen or so players signed their caps and gave them to him, which made his day, if not his year. One thing about the senior players worldwide... when it comes to any charity they always put their hands up and contribute. It makes me extremely proud to be a part of that. The sponsors were very excited about my gesture towards Albert and said that I was welcome to come back to play at anytime.

The following year, 1992, the United States Senior team of eight players were to play against a team of senior players from the rest of the world in what was called the Chrysler Cup, in Sarasota, Florida.

Having just beaten Palmer, Player, Horton, Charles and many other top senior players in the Senior Open, I thought it was a forgone conclusion that I would be included in that team, particularly as my brother-in-law was also the captain of the rest of the world team. When I asked him why I wasn't considered to play in this tournament, but Tommy Horton was, his reply was that the other players thought that Horton was a better player than I was. In later years he subsequently proved he was, but he certainly wasn't the better player at the time. While he was an absolute gentleman off the golf course, his language was diabolical and his behaviour generally atrocious whenever he played a game of golf. He really wasn't a nice man. Two other guys, Bruce Devlin and Billy Dunk, who were also chosen to be part of the team were playing poorly at the time and the fact that they had both been chosen over me made me extremely unhappy – I wasn't asking for favours, just acknowledgement.

When I queried Gary about these decisions, he told me that it was not up to him to decide. I thought that was a bullshit story as it was always up to the captain to choose the team. I was proved right, when it came to the Presidents Cup a few years later, when K. J. Choi, who was way ahead of Trevor Immelman on world rankings, wasn't picked for the team. Gary had chosen his friend Immelman above Choi, which really was a disgrace. When the media asked him how he could do this, his answer was that as the captain, he decided and he would choose whoever he thought was the best for the team.

Later that same year, Gary secured a Coca-Cola sponsorship for a tournament in honour of Nelson Mandela. Many great sportsmen from all different types of sport were invited to play in this charity golf tournament. As my record at that time was very good and better than most, I was again waiting with bated breath to be invited to play in this prestigious event. John Fourie, who has only beaten me once over a ten-year period, got an invite each and every year ahead of me. When I phoned Mark Player, the organiser of the tournament, to ask what was going on, he told me it was the sponsor's decision. However, when I phoned the sponsors demanding some answers, they told me the selections were made by Mark and Gary.

I suppose I should have been grateful for later receiving a personal invite from Mark Player to come and watch the tournament if I wanted to, but all this did was rub salt into an already painful wound, and I declined the invitation.

Chapter Eighteen

PLAYING WITH THE CHAMPS

WHILE PLAYING in the Swedish Senior Open in Copenhagen, something out of the ordinary happened that I will never forget. We were on the ninth hole and I hit my drive and walked off the tee to quickly relieve myself. While standing behind a tree, about a metre in front of me was a deer laying on the grass about to give birth. I stood there in awe as I watched this miracle of life. She was not fazed by my presence and continued to do what came naturally. My team mates were screaming their heads off for me to join them, but I kept as still and quiet, as I possibly could. Fifteen minutes later, the little fawn got up and steadily got stronger as she moved away with her mommy. When I related this awesome story to my fellow players, they were mad as all hell because I hadn't called them over to share in the experience. They were very envious of this once-in-a-lifetime experience. It really is true what they say, you know: 'Playing golf really does beat any day at the office.'

A couple of years later we played the Senior Open at Royal County Down. I really loved this course and although I never won, I did manage to finish third and fourth in various tournaments.

One year in the third round, I shot 69 in windy and extremely difficult conditions. At the end of the round, I went to the clubhouse and was having tea and scones, when Duncan Lindsey Smith came and sat with me. Duncan was a famous South African sportsman; having played cricket and golf for South Africa, he was one of very few double Springboks. He was also a very fine senior golfer. He told me he had just walked the whole eighteen holes, watching me play and that he was in awe of the way I conducted myself and played my golf. Then he paid me the biggest compliment of all when he said that because of this and the way I played, it was no wonder he could never beat me.

As the winner of the British Senior Open, I was invited to play in the Fuji Grandslam tournament in Japan. In addition to the air ticket, the IMG also told me they would be paying me $10,000 as well as covering all additional expenses. A week before leaving, the sponsors called me to say that they would only be paying me $2,000 as they were also sending Lee Trevino to compete in Japan. He had just turned 49, as in Japan you are one year old when you are born, which made him 50 years old according to their customs, therefore qualified to play. I didn't mind at all, because Lee was a good friend, a great golfer and known as a great entertainer; like me, everyone welcomed him on the tour.

In 1992 I was invited to Scottsdale Arizona at Tradition, Desert Mountain, which was to become the fourth major tournament on the PGA tour after the US Open, the US PGA and the British Senior Open. It was run and organised by a great man called Lyle Anderson, who was a huge property developer and later became one of my very good friends. I arrived there five days before the tournament started and enjoyed the generosity of the sponsors as everything from food, accommodation and drinks were on the house.

The first week I was there, I was invited to the Champions' dinner, so called as the players on this tour were all winners of a major tournament. As it was my first appearance here, it was my turn to make a speech in front of my idols of many years – Sam Snead, Arnold Palmer, Lee Trevino, Gary Player, Jack Nicklaus and Bob Charles, to name a few.

I was extremely nervous when they called my name, but managed to stand up and make a speech. I started off by saying that for me to make a speech and for them to have to sit there listening to me was an honour and privilege. I also told them a joke, and how I had admired each and everyone of them for many a year. Jack Nicklaus came to me after the dinner and told me how much he enjoyed the speech and that it was one of the most entertaining he had ever listened to.

I ended up going back to Desert Mountain for the next eight years, mostly taking my sons Bobby Junior and Bradley to caddy for me while I was there. Isobel also came with and caddied on occasion for me as well. Over the years I fell madly in love with Arizona, particularly Desert Mountain in Scottsdale. I met a lot of great people and still have contact with most of them.

One of the highlights of the tournament was when it snowed the night before, which meant that play was cancelled. On this occasion, Lyle Anderson asked me if I could put on a golf clinic for about 500 guests who were there to watch us play. They arranged the 500 chairs around the driving range tee, when everyone was seated, I joined them and as I looked up saw a smiling Lee Trevino standing on a walkway behind the chairs.

My opening statement was: 'Good Morning, ladies and gentlemen. Most of you may think of me as Gary Player's brother-in-law. Let me make it absolutely clear... Gary Player is *my* brother-in-law.'

Lee Trevino laughed and shouted, 'Guys, you are in good hands. I am on my way to practise.'

I kept them entertained for three or four hours. Unlike most clinics I got nearly all of the guests onto the tee and gave them each a few good tips. Years later I was still asked by some to do another clinic, because they had enjoyed it so much. A big feather in my cap. Lyle Anderson was delighted and thanked me for doing such a great job.

By 1996, I was back in South Africa when I received a phone call from the SA Soccer Union. They wanted me to have a game with Sir Bobby Charlton, as he was here for the African Cup of Nations and South Africa was in the finals. I arranged to meet him at the River Club Golf Club, a fantastic private golf club in Johannesburg. We met and had a great round of golf; he turned out to be an absolute gentleman and a genuinely nice guy. After the round we had a couple of drinks and something to eat. While we were having lunch he asked if I would be interested in a ticket to attend his private box with Pele and other soccer dignitaries. I thanked him very profusely for the invite but told him that while I myself was unfortunately not really a avid fan and lover of soccer, I knew a man who had worked for me for ten years was an absolutely soccer-mad fan, who would be over the moon for such a rare opportunity.

This soccer fanatic, Joe Chuena, was beside himself when I handed him the ticket. The event was taking place two days later and I told him he would have to wear a jacket and tie, but that everything else would be paid for. However, I made sure he had at least R300 in his pocket, then he asked me whether he was allowed to shout if South Africa scored. I said, 'You can scream and shout as loud as you want.'

He had a fantastic time and even more so as South Africa won the Cup. He phoned me afterwards to thank me again and asked for a few days off from his job, as he had met this gorgeous waitress and was madly in love. He came back to work three days later with a smile that no one could wipe off his face. Before Sir Bobby went back to England he gave me his personal contact numbers and said that I had an open invitation to visit him whenever I was in England.

A year later, a son of a friend of mine, Jonathan Friedman, had his 21st birthday and his wish was to see the Springboks play England at Twickenham, as well as watch Manchester United play a match. When I phoned Sir Bobby, to ask if it would be possible to secure tickets, I spoke to his secretary who assured me that she would pass on the message, as he was out of town. He called me back a couple of hours later and confirmed that he could arrange it for me. I gave his number to Jonathan and told him to call him as soon as they were in the UK. Needless to say, Sir Bobby, true to his word, went out of his way to ensure that Jonathan received what has to be the best 21st birthday present any soccer-mad youngster could receive.

The following year, I played in a big Senior Tournament just south of Chester, near Manchester and in the first round as I was walking towards the sixth tee, I felt this hand on my shoulder. I looked up and it was Sir Bobby. He said he had watched me play the first three holes and he had not wanted to break my concentration, but would I have a drink with him once I finished my round? At the time I was playing with two English golfers with three English caddies and as Sir Bobby walked away, they looked at me in amazement, wanting to know how I knew him. Jokingly, I told them that we had been friends for years. This must have impressed the socks off them because Sir Bobby is as famous in England as Babe Ruth was in America.

Chapter Nineteen

BENDING THE RULES

A T THIS point, I think it's fair and necessary to mention some bending of the rules and some outright cheating that I saw happen on the course during my golfing career.

Back in the early 1960s, Harold Henning played most of his golf in Europe or in South Africa. Although Harold was going through a bad spell at the time, to my mind, he was always a brilliant player and certainly one of the best that South Africa has ever produced.

Although Harold hadn't been playing well, he managed to secure an invite to play in a tournament at Moorpark Golf Club in London, after one of the other qualifying players broke his leg. The money was good as even the player who came last received £1,000 – a very tidy sum in those days.

It so happened that there was a special prize for the first hole in one, which Harold, in true Henning style, aced on the eighteenth hole. The prize money was £10,000 which was an absolute fortune. Realising that he would have to pay a considerable amount of tax on his winnings, two of his buddies were there as a caddy and manager, Brian Lundy and Dennis Hutchinson. They put a plan together so that he would not have to pay tax on this windfall. They suggested he divided the money between all three of them. After the dust settled, the money was given back to Harold, with him giving each of them a couple of hundred pounds for their trouble. Double standards? I would bloody well think so, when you consider that these were the very same people who had sat in a boardroom, condemned me for cheating and barred me from playing for two years.

I spoke to Harold a week or so later, telling him that I couldn't understand why he preferred to play in Europe, as the money in the US was so much better. The following year he took my advice and played in the US and never returned to play in Europe again. In the years to follow, of all the pros I was friends with, I can genuinely say he was my best friend. Come to think of it, all of the Henning brothers were wonderful guys and we shared a lifelong friendship. Sadly, both Harold and his brother Graham have passed away.

There is, of course, much more to life than just cheating the taxman. Although I'd like to say that honesty prevailed on the golf course, sadly this wasn't always the case.

One year on the 72nd hole of the British Open, Gary Player hit his ball against the clubhouse wall. The only way he could play the ball was left-handed with his putter. The ball was lying very sandy and he proceeded to put the putter behind the ball and scrape a path. This is totally illegal. He then putted the ball onto the green and eventually won the tournament by two or three strokes. Quite amazing that the R&A committee stood around and nobody brought him to task. With the world watching and the cameras rolling, he was not penalised and a blind eye was turned to this blatant discrepancy. To my knowledge he sometimes got away with murder; just ask Tom Watson.

One year in the Greensborough Open in North Carolina, I was playing with Bruce Crampton. There was a stream at the 17th, running diagonally across the fairway. The water was quite deep, although not very wide. The hazard had stakes on the outside with grassy banks, from where the ball could still be played. Crampton had hit his ball into about three feet of water, under a bridge. He called for a ruling, saying that he wanted a play of the ball, which was not possible as the bridge was in the way of his swing. He wanted a drop. He got to drop the ball away from the bridge on the grassy bank, where he hit the ball and made a par. If that is not legal cheating, I don't know what is!

Years later, Tiger Woods, playing in Phoenix, had just landed a ball next to a huge boulder. The rules at that time stated you could remove any loose obstacle, be it a leaf or stone, away from your ball. Not the least bothered by this, he called six or seven strong young male spectators to move a 1,000-pound boulder out of the way and proceeded to hit his ball on the green unhindered... and later win the tournament. I regard this as extremely unfair, given that the next player who found himself in the same predicament probably wouldn't have the benefit of spectators moving a huge boulder for him and would have to drop a shot. The reason I do not like this ruling is because usually the famous names benefit from certain rules and the 'hotdog' pros are left out. For the record, the term 'hotdog golfer' refers to lesser-known players who come up behind the more famous names. When a spectator asks a friend who that particular golfer is, the reply will invariably be, 'I don't know... let's go get a hotdog!'

I don't want to imply or say that I was a goody two-shoes, but on several occasions I called a penalty shot on myself and in my forty-five years of playing professionally, I never ever heard another professional call a penalty shot when he moved the ball. I did, however, sometimes hear in the media that Lee Trevino, Jack Nicklaus and Tom Watson had called a penalty shot, but never when I was around. Makes you think, doesn't it?

Years ago, the story was that one of South Africa's well-known golfing personalities allegedly ordered and received about R300,000 worth of golfing merchandise from one of the agents. He apparently resold all of the golfing equipment, without paying the agent, then left the country. The story goes that he spent two or three years in California and then returned – clean as a whistle and the matter was never discussed again. From what I've heard no money was ever handed over for the goods, yet today, he is still regarded as a well-respected personality in the golfing fraternity, sporting a photo in the SA Golf Hall of Fame.

Another South African golf pro, who is also known as being an excellent golf-coach, was caught stealing antique snuff boxes. He quickly left the country for the

US and although he never returned to this country, after twenty or thirty years, his name is proudly displayed in the SA Golf Hall of Fame. My father, who won the South African PGA Championship three times, was runner-up to Bobby Locke twice in the South African Open and who incidentally also won a couple of PGA tournaments, is not in this Golf Hall of Fame. Apart from the fact that he was a decent, honest man and undoubtedly one of the finest golf coaches in South Africa, the South African golfing authorities have never recognised his talent or achievements. I have heard recently that both my father and I are under consideration; however, they are presently giving preference to golfers who had success overseas and in South Africa. What! Have I been invisible all this time?

All of this leaves a bitter taste in my mouth and I wonder how some people seemingly get away with everything while the rest of us sit silently from the sidelines watching.

Chapter Twenty

ULCERS AND TARAS BULBA

THE SENIOR Tour started to grow big at this time and I was able to win a number of tournaments. I won the Sir Lawrence Batley tournament in Huddersfield, England twice, in 1997 and 1998. This proved to be a good year as I also won the Senior Swiss Open in Badragaz, Switzerland. Interestingly enough, the evening before the tournament, they had a media conference at the five star Badragaz Hotel. It was sponsored by Credit Suisse, and like most sporting events sponsored by them, was very well organised on a grand and lavish scale. At the conference they asked Tommy Horton what his chances were the next day. His answered that he thought he could beat me. They then asked me the same question, my cheeky remark was that with the way I was playing, Tommy would only be able to beat me 'if hell freezes over'. Arrogant, you may think, but keeping it positive, I thought.

I played very well, without ever being in trouble. The course suited my game because it was short and narrow. I beat Tommy by three shots.

Two weeks later, I was staying with Gary Hughes at Heathrow, Orlando, where we had invested a lot of money in the breeding of ostriches. At the time, we had bought about two and a half thousand birds. Unfortunately for me, he turned out to be a conman, selling the same ostriches to a number of different people. Some time after my visit he filed for bankruptcy and skipped Orlando. My loss came to at least $30,000.

While I was staying with him, I was on the so-called 'Jack Nicklaus cabbage diet' and after my experience, I would strongly advise against anyone going on such a diet. However, in my case, it was also a recipe for disaster, considering that I had suffered with a duodenal ulcer for many years.

One evening we went to the local bar and had a couple of scotches. As I got back to my room a few hours later, I collapsed on my bed, haemorrhaging from my mouth among other places. I called Gary Hughes and he rushed me to the nearest hospital. It turned out that the Sanford Hospital was one of the best hospitals I have ever had the (mis)fortune of visiting and for the next ten hours I was given VIP treatment. My vitals and blood tests were done every 15 minutes. In the morning I was taken to the operating theatre where an Indian doctor was going to perform a procedure on me. However, he was a very talkative fellow, praising and talking non-stop about Sachin Tendulkar, the great Indian cricket player and the game of cricket which he loved. Although, feeling like death, I obliged him by talking about his hero, as I was also a big fan and lover of the game. I was still lying on the gurney when a nurse came to me and said she wanted to spray an anaesthetic into my throat for the doctor to place the gastrometer into my stomach.

As I was lying there thinking that there was no way they could put that thing down my throat without me gagging, the doctor walked up to me with an X-ray in his hand. I asked him what it was and he said it was a picture of my stomach. I said, 'How the hell did you get that?' He explained that the nurse had slipped the medical equipment down my throat, when I opened my mouth for the spray. The X-ray showed my stomach was filled with blood. He had managed to cauterise the ulcer to stop the bleeding, but if the bleeding didn't stop, I'd be facing a life-threatening emergency.

That afternoon my haemoglobin shot up, when Gary Hughes visited me and told me that the hospital was costing $7,000 per day. When the doctor came to see me later in the day, I told him that I was going home in the morning. He told me that I would have to stay there for at least two weeks and if I left the next day, I could die. I retorted that if I stayed there for two weeks more at $7,000 a day, it was 'going to kill me anyway'.

He did allow me to go home, but advised me to stay in bed and have enough rest in order to fully recuperate. Amazingly, one of the directors of the hospital came to visit me the next day. I assumed he was there to collect on my hospital debt, as they hadn't given me a bill when I'd been discharged. He said that because of my social security number and because I was a senior citizen, all they required was $500. Let me tell you, I never wrote out a cheque faster in my entire life.

Ten days later, I went to Charlotte, North Carolina, to play in the Payne Webber tournament at Piper Glen. This was an Arnold Palmer Golf course and also one of my favourite golf courses in the world. As I was still weak after my stint in hospital, I played very poorly. I played with Tony Jacklin and posted my highest score ever of 83.

The following week, I was due to play in the first professional golf tournament ever to be held in Turkey: the first Turkish Senior Open in Antalya, Turkey, south of Istanbul. I flew from Charlotte to Heathrow, where I had a connecting flight to Istanbul. When I looked out the window at the airport I saw the orange tail of the South African Airways plane parked next to the Turkish Airways plane and, in my weakened state, could not decide whether I should go home or on to Turkey.

From my schooldays, I had always had a desire to visit Turkey, as I was fascinated by the stories of Taras Bulba, a Cossack colonel who fought against the Turks. So I made my decision to get on that plane and went to Antalya, Turkey. It turned out to be a very, very wise decision – I won the Turkish Open by six strokes.

It so happened that I'd spent the day before the tournament hitting golf balls and picking up a few tips from my good South African friend, Tienie Britz, who had won the South African PGA twice during the '60s. After the win I gave him £250 as payment for his more than helpful advice.

Another one of my much-loved golf courses is the Sunningdale Golf Club in Surrey, England. They have two courses, aptly named the Old and the New. The Old

Course has a special place in my heart, as it is where I played my first golf tournament in Britain in 1958 in the Bowmaker Pro-Amateur. Obviously, I was an amateur, as I was only 17 at the time and my professional partner was Sebastian Miguel, one of the famous Miguel brothers and two of the finest players from Spain.

They weren't the only pleasant Spanish people I had ever met and this book wouldn't be complete without a special mention of another, unforgettable Spaniard, Seve Ballesteros, whom I had the great honour of knowing.

I was 33 and he was 17 years old when we first met and played in the PGA at the Wanderers Golf Club in 1974. I could recognise a whole lot of talent when I saw it, but he unfortunately did not make the cut and after two rounds he came to thank me for helping him over those two days. He was, as everyone knows, in for much bigger things. Over the next thirty years whenever we saw each other he always used to greet me in his friendly Spanish way, with a jovial hug and a kiss on the cheek. It was with great sadness that I heard about his passing at the age of 54, after a long battle with cancer. He was and still is a real inspiration to many players.

I played the British PGA championship at Sunningdale quite a few times and one particular year, a fantastic duel unfolded when I played with Welshman Brian Huggett, who was a great golfer. Many years before in 1962, when I won the German Open in Hamburg, I played with him on the final day, beating him by one stroke. Now it was his turn to beat me by one stroke. We were firm friends and always had great rivalry when it came to golf and the Springbok and Welsh rugby teams.

The tournament was sponsored by the Forte Hotel group owned by the Forte brothers, who always put on a good tournament. What made it even more pleasant was that I got to stay with John and Patsy Boardman, good friends of mine. John was on the board of the Royal & Ancient Committee before his retirement. We had some really awesome evenings as they both had a great sense of humour and we shared many laughs and a good few scotches together.

I also had the pleasure of meeting the famous Sir Douglas Bader, a war veteran who had lost both his legs at the beginning of the Second World War while flying in the Royal Air force. His story is legendary and despite having what most would consider a serious disability, he convinced the Air Force that he was still able to fly. He went on to fly fighter planes and even managed to escape wearing artificial legs when he was shot down later in the war.

I went back to Japan again in 2000, when ten players got invited to play in Tokyo in the Jurin Open. The course was designed by Pete Dye and was the toughest he had ever built. The first prize was $30,000. I was not putting or playing too well and one of my Japanese friends, Hiro, gave me a putting tip, which did wonders for my game.

It was supposed to be a 36-hole tournament, but the first round was rained out and it subsequently became an 18-hole challenge. I shot seventy that day. I didn't know what the leading score was when I walked up to the 18th hole, which happened to be the most difficult part of the course because there were water hazards everywhere.

About 30 yards short of the green with the pin three metres from the water on the left, I played one of the most courageous shots in my life and hit it a foot from the hole. Then I putted to win the $30,000. What was so incredible about this was it was the exact amount that I needed in order to finish the driving range that I was building back in South Africa.

Along with the money, I won a magnificent crystal vase as well as another golf-bag, golf-shoes, caps, shirts, balls and all kinds of golfing equipment from the sponsors. One of my friends told me that I would have to pay a huge amount of tax to get all of this back to South Africa. I had two golf bags, one very heavy bag and a small carry-on bag – all of it weighing in at about 100 kilogrammes, excluding the enormous crystal trophy which I had to carry.

I was flying Cathay Pacific from Hong Kong to Johannesburg. When I got to the airport there was about twenty weigh-in counters. I had kept aside a Foot Joy glove, PING cap and a box of Titleist golf balls. As I got to the very pretty ladies at the counters, I asked each one whether they played golf. As I got to the third counter, the lady told me her husband not only played golf – he adored the game. I told her that I was doing a promotion on Titleist, PING and Foot Joy and gave her a glove, cap and balls. To my enormous relief she was so ecstatic that she checked all my luggage through, refusing to charge me an extra cent for excess baggage.

The problem, however, was far from over as I still had to pass through customs at Johannesburg International Airport. Scheming once again, I walked to the red line for something to declare. When I got to the customs official, I told him that I had just won this big tournament in Japan, and asked him whether I needed to pay any duty on this huge crystal trophy in my hands. He requested to see the trophy and I dutifully and with a great amount of fanfare took it out of the box, he held it up, admired it and told me it was absolutely magnificent and I would not have to pay. He waved me through the exit doors, not even glancing at the fully laden trolley behind me.

I was so happy about not having to pay yet again and wanted to share my good luck with some underprivileged kids who I had been teaching at the Verwey driving range. They were over the moon with all the goodies I distributed amongst them the next day.

On reflection I found Japan to be a fantastic country. I adore the discipline of the people, the cleanliness of the cities, as well as their competence and business acumen. Unfortunately, I have never been back, but hope that I am able to still do so in the future.

Chapter Twenty-One

BAD DECISIONS

IN 2001, I was playing in the British Senior Open at Royal County Down, when Isobel flew up to join me. Over the next couple of days, I noticed that Isobel was not her usual self. She was an introvert, but for some reason had become even more quiet and kept to herself. I was very involved in the tour, finishing third and winning a big fat cheque. After the tournament, I put her on the plane at Heathrow, as I was to play one more tournament before flying back to South Africa. When I arrived home a week later, I was in for some unexpected and completely devastating news. Isobel told me that she still loved me, but not like she used to and that she wanted a divorce. Completely taken by surprise and shocked to the core, I could not believe what was happening and desperately tried to make sense of it all.

On further investigation, I established that a woman had been visiting her every day at the house, while I was gone. I made enquiries and found out that she was well-known in gay circles and had been friends with Isobel for some time. Isobel denied that she had a relationship with her, said that this woman was only a friend and that this had nothing to do with her decision to ask for a divorce.

A friend of mine, Peter Gotz, told me that he knew a great marriage counsellor in Plettenberg Bay in the Eastern Cape and that maybe it would help if we flew down to speak to her. I could have very easily stopped this strange relationship, as the other woman turned out to be a coward of note. She denied everything when I confronted her over the phone. Apparently a friend of hers had also told her that she was playing with fire by starting an affair with Bobby Verwey's wife.

We flew to Plettenberg Bay, but it was a complete and utter waste of time, as her mind was back in Johannesburg and she did not even begin to commit to discussions with the counsellor. I had to face reality – my marriage was on the rocks… there was no chance of a reconciliation.

The two of us went down to the river-mouth near the beach in Plettenberg Bay to have a heart-to-heart talk. While sitting there talking, I looked up and saw a whale leisurely swimming upstream, a mere ten metres away. It was a totally surreal experience, the sight of this whale swimming past us will be engraved in my memory for as long as I live.

When we returned to Johannesburg, I immediately moved out and went to stay with my mother, who was understandably upset. Isobel continued to deny that she was having an affair and told me to stop telling everyone she was, as it was defamatory. As it turned out, her own mother was so devastated that she never went back to visit her at the house and died not long after. The woman, an accountant, moved in with her two days later and they have been together ever since.

The divorce hit me very hard. Isobel and I had so much in common and I naively believed we were going to grow old together. I remained in denial for a long time and it took me around three to four years to get over her.

I was upset, humiliated and more than a little embarrassed and wanted to remove myself from the unpleasant saga as quickly as possible, so made little fuss and signed all of the legal documents. She sold the property I had poured my heart and soul and more than a bit of money into, for around R24 million six or seven years after the divorce. I sent her a text message at the time asking her about reimbursing me all the money I had spent on the place and only received a caustic 'Ha ha ha' message back. Karma is a bitch, I told her and never heard from her again.

Later I heard, she bought a riding school in the Natal Midlands and moved there with her new 'friend'. I hope she can find the happiness she was looking for with all her undeserved millions. Sadly, I lost a good friend in Peter Gotz, too, as I also never heard from him again. The fact that Isobel is his daughter's godmother may have something to do with it.

And then, if it wasn't bad enough that I lost my wife to another woman, I also lost a damn good caddy.

It wasn't the only devastating occurrence that happened that year.

My mother, Christine, whom I loved dearly, developed a pain in her stomach, which was at first misdiagnosed. By the time they found the problem, the cancer in her womb had spread to such an extent that it was inoperable. She was a very strong woman, an absolute lady, who still played golf at the age of 84. She was well loved wherever she went and had made countless friends when she travelled around the world with Gary and Vivienne.

She might not have gone through the hell the way she did, had the cancer been diagnosed earlier. She was incredibly brave and although she fought this dreadful illness with all her might, she sadly passed away a year later. It was an enormous loss to all who loved her. We miss her and will always remember what a wonderful woman, mother and grandmother she was.

Over the next ten years, I still played, golf, albeit mediocre golf. At the age of sixty-two I was no longer able to compete against the young, up-and-coming golfers in South Africa. I was having a lot of trouble with my left wrist and eventually, in an effort to relieve the pain a surgeon operated, partially fusing the joint. As things turned out I could still play golf, but the pain never went away. As one surgeon explained to me, it was arthritis and that I would always have the pain when I played in colder weather.

In my last senior year, 2005, I played at Wentworth in London at the beginning of the British winter and ended up battling in the freezing conditions. I was playing very poorly and decided to withdraw in the last round – I never played in another tournament again.

I had built the Verwey Driving Range at Fourways, Johannesburg in 2000 and opened it in 2001. All three of my sons helped with the running of the Range. It was a 20-acre property with a 500 square metre clubhouse and a huge bar. Unfortunately, it was built near a major road going between Johannesburg and Diepsloot which was in desperate need of an upgrade; it also didn't help that the local authority allowed another driving range to open just up the road. I focused on offering free golfing lessons to the underprivileged kids who lived in nearby townships. However, my profits soon started to slip when my paying customers, in an effort to avoid the bad road that led to my range, started using the other range, which was closer to town. I sold the driving range after eleven years and decided to retire.

After receiving advice from one of my doctors, who stated that I should have a plate inserted into my wrist if I ever wanted to play golf again, I jumped at the opportunity. I underwent a full fusion on my wrist in 2010. I have made a few mistakes in my life, but this was by far one of the most foolish decisions I have ever made. My wrist is now completely fused and I am not able to turn my hand to grip a club properly. Sadly, this means that unless I start to play left or one-handed, my playing days are forever over.

A few wise words from this old golf pro, if I may. When I think of the great Tiger Woods and his back problems, this is my penny's worth. In my opinion he swung way too hard and had a very big head dip, which put too much pressure on his back, hence the problems he had in later years. I do condemn his former coaches for not rectifying this. To correct this problem is quite simple. You have to hit balls off a foot high (300mm) golf tee, from your pitching wedge to your driver at half pace. That will sort any head dip out very quickly. One of the top lady golf-pros, Paula Cremer, has the same bad head dip. None of her coaches have helped her in fixing this.

A final tip to every golfer. Grip the club lightly and never swing with more than 60 to 70 per cent of your power. You will find your game improving immediately.

Chapter Twenty-Two

DISAPPOINTMENTS AND REGRETS

T HERE WERE a few things that disappointed me when I got to the US Senior Tour after winning the Senior British Open in 1991. As I chatted with some of the other players, I was under the wrong impression that they had started the Senior Tour for the older players in order to assist them to make some money, as a financial backup or to form some sort of a pension scheme. It was most upsetting that they allowed other players from outside the US to also participate in the Tour.

I suggested to the members of the Senior Tour committee that senior players from the rest of the world should only be allowed on the tour if they had previously supported the US Tour, as well as having played in at least a hundred tournaments in the US. Regretfully, this never happened and as such the US Senior Tour grew at a much faster rate than the European Senior Tour.

It was only because of Andy Stubbs, who was tournament director of the European Senior Tour at the time and did a fantastic job promoting the Senior Tour in Europe by finding sponsors and golfers, that the European Tour became so successful.

By the time the US Tour decided to form a pension fund for senior golfers, the players were already earning so much money that they really didn't need a pension. It was the predecessors, the golf pioneers, Harold Henning and others like myself, who never had the terrific financial opportunities that our younger counterparts have enjoyed, who needed the money.

There are numerous players from the 'fifties, 'sixties and 'seventies, the forerunners to the US Tour – great players, major tournament winners, legends in their own time – who are now in dire need of some sort of financial support. Some of the top players, who must have a fortune in pension money coming to them, would not stand up at any meeting to support some fund for the forgotten legends of their time. A number of the great players of old have died penniless because the PGA did not look after them as they should have.

A pledge of around $5,000 a month plus some sort of medical insurance could have and would have had an enormous impact on these players' quality of life and yet, although the PGA makes millions every year, they have chosen to forget those who basically put the game of golf on the map. As a foreign player who supported the US Tour for ten years and played in hundreds of tour events, this has always been a thorn in my side.

I had a few driving ranges and coaching jobs after my career ended, so fortunately did not end up penniless, but it would have been very different had I been appreciated for my contribution after spending 60 years on the golf course, come rain or shine, and walking thousands of miles for the measly remuneration we got so many years ago.

My many cut-glass trophies and unusable glass candy bowls on the mantelpiece are really a mockery of what we went through. Most of the time, we had to pay our own way and sometimes it was a struggle to afford a flight or decent accommodation. I personally spent hundreds of hours playing in pro-ams, charming potential sponsors and their guests, never mind the countless hours on the road in a rental car, with three active boys and a tired wife, trying to reach the next tournament and hopefully earn a few dollars, which appears to have gone unrecognised by the PGA and other governing bodies.

Driving across America for an average of six or seven hundred miles a week for about seven months of the year, in order to get to the next tournament, sometimes as much as fifteen hundred miles away; changing diapers in the car, feeding hungry children and looking for the cheapest cafeteria: these were all part of the touring pro's life in those days. We put up with a lot and I have to admire the passion and dedication of my fellow players who struggled through it all.

This was a way of life for me and my family for the best part of seven years. Yes, you could say that I was fortunate to see America from Boston to Seattle and

Miami to San Diego and everywhere else in between. However, reaching your destination tired and with very little time to prepare for the tournament was rough on us all; but apart from all the hardships, we enjoyed life.

Today, there are top players in their 20s and 30s who have their own jets and can afford million-dollar mansions all over the world. I do not deny that there are some of today's champions who donate millions to their chosen charities and contribute immensely to the game of golf, but I do think that charity should start at home. I am, however, proud of what I have achieved and would do it a million times over again, because of the love I have for the silly little game called golf.

At the age of 74, I look back at an awesome life. I have been blessed in so many ways and the highlights definitely outweigh the lows.

My sons have always continued to make me proud. Bobby Junior is the golf coach for the Moroccan team as well as the Royal Moroccan Family in Marrakech. He travels all over the world and carries the Verwey legacy with him. He qualified for and is very excited about playing in his first Senior Open. His son, Nicholas, has inherited his father's sporting genes and is showing great promise as a cricketer. His other two young sons, Luke and Ryan, live in Florida, US with their mother and he visits them as often as he can.

My son, Brad, is also a golf pro, and married to Tessa, a boutique owner, but only plays golf for his own pleasure. They live in a sleepy little town on the South Coast of KZN called Southbroom. He has so much potential, but sadly has no desire to follow in his father's footsteps. Maybe, just maybe, he will get the urge to join Bobby Junior on the Senior Tour one day. To have one son play the fairways where I played is incredible, but to have two of my three sons follow in my footsteps would exceed my wildest expectations. An old man can dream, can't he?

My youngest son, Darren, is a scratch handicap golfer; he stayed an amateur and plays with friends occasionally, but prefers the wheeling and dealing at his second-hand business in Johannesburg. He is father to two beautiful girls, Tayla and Megan, and is a dedicated husband to his wife Susan.

I now have Nina, a wonderful woman in my life, who has coloured my world and makes me want to live to 102. If it wasn't for her, perhaps this book would never have been written. She keeps me honest, healthy, and reasonably well-mannered! Unfortunately, I still chew on ice cubes, get up to snack in the middle of the night and mess all over the place and leave cupboard doors open, but I am trying hard to mend my ways.

As always, I still love to talk to people. So, come on over, we can have a chat over a big rump steak and a double scotch – short glass, lots of ice and water on the side.

This is Bobby Verwey… over for now, but far from out.

ACHIEVEMENTS, HIGHLIGHTS

3rd Canadian Open, 3rd Texas Open, 2nd Minnesota
Open '67, 4th Hawaiian Open, 5th Azalea Open, 3rd
Oklahoma Open, 5th Oklahoma Open, 4th Buick Open,
5th Portland Open, 3rd British Sr Open '01, Runner up
Forte Sr PGA Open '93.

Finished 25 times in the top five in Europe and South
Africa between 1960 and 1970.

Winner French Amateur Open 1958
Winner German Amateur Open 1958
Winner German Open 1962
Winner Dunlop Open 1964
Winner Almedan Open US Tour 1965
Winner Transvaal Open 4 times
Winner Western Province Open 1967
Winner Transkei Open 1975
Winner British Senior Open 1991
Winner Lawrence Battley 1992, 1998
Winner Turkish Open 1996
Winner Credit Swiss Senior Open 1998
Winner Jurin Open Tokyo 2001,
Third in South African Open 1972
Runner up to Gary Player South African Open 1976

Runner up to Gary Player in Sun City Classic 1980

Twice topped Order of Merit in SA

Represented South Africa in the World Cup 1978 Hawaii and 1980 Bogota, Colombia

FAMILY ACHIEVEMENTS

JOCK VERWEY, 15 holes in one
CHRISTINE VERWEY, 3 holes in one
VIVIENNE VERWEY, 4 holes in one of which 2 was in the same round…
BOBBY VERWEY, 17 holes in one

An unbelievable achievement for a family of four!